THE
DELTA BLUES

To:
Dr. Kevin Rice M.D,
Best Wishes
&
May God Bless

Mildred Wells-Dunn

THE
DELTA BLUES

We Have Come A Long Way

Mildred Wells-Dunn

To order additional copies of this book, contact:
Xlibris Corporation
1-888-795-4274
www.Xlibris.com
Orders@Xlibris.com
20338

CONTENTS

This book is dedicated to my sons, TyJuan and Jarvis; brother Charlie Thomas, who is one hundred and two years old; and especially to Aubrey Louis Wells, another nephew, who suffers from cuts and hits to his head–causing the family to come forward. The world was informed of the injustice and they came to Tunica and found gold. Mr. Aubrey Wells, the world thanks you and we love you. As I write this, tears are in my eyes.

Bridging the Gap Between
the Home, School, Church, and Community,
with Emphasis on Putting Parents
Back to Being Parents
and Lowering the Stress Level in the Home

Robinsonville Town

Tunica County, Mississippi

Mildred Wells-Dunn

Mildred Wells-Dunn, mother, widow, teacher, bishop, writer, community helper, pastor, farmer, activist, president of the neighborhood, chef, and C.E.O. of Bridging the Gap Between the Home, School, Church and Community.

Foreword

Why Not Remember?

*M*ost of us don't have anything to build on because we have forgotten our foundation. Some of us want to start from today, and you know, your roots started yesterday. To build in mid-air is falling success. Don't be ashamed to dig up your roots; you might find a mountain instead of a hill. It's okay to remember what grandma or grandpa said or did. They can tell you who their parents and grandparents were. We have more history around us than we care to admit. It doesn't make you old to know, just wise. Don't allow your parents and grandparents to pass this way and not share what they know or heard with you. Just think how far behind we would be if we had not built on the things our foremothers and forefathers did. Trees are the substances of seeds planted, and so are we. Our ancestors planted the seeds so we could live a good life. We are thinking about the hourglass, that is our key for motivation, and where would we be if we didn't have something to motivate us and keep us in a time frame?

Acknowledgments

My first thanks is to God for allowing me to continue writing through my illness, the loss of my husband, family members, and other things that betided me. I have written for a long time, and I understand that if it had not been for the love and care of others, it would have been impossible for me to get this far.

I thank my neighbors, Mr. Keith and Mrs. Gloria Williams; my sons, TyJuan and Jarvis; Mr. Charles Tatum, Mrs. Helen Tatum-Wells, Mrs. Robyn Weiss, Mrs. Christine Phillips, Mr. C. P. Owen III, Mr. Shay Leatherman; and all of those who listen while I attempt to explain the points of life in the Delta.

Mr. Williams spent countless hours guiding me through bridging the gap and works. Mrs. Phillips also burned the midnight oil, and I am glad she had her grandson—Brian, I believe, is his name—to keep her going.

If I am never paid for some things, I am just sorry, because some things may come to pass—what has been and what will be. Bridging the gap is found in the Bible; the Delta Blues is what I lived. I want the up and coming generation to know what it was and how it can be. If this book is published by Xlibris, I thank you in advance for a job well done.

Introduction

Since blacks first arrived in the Delta as sharecroppers from all over, thousands upon thousands have come up with good ideas. There were a few white sharecroppers in different places, but sharecropping was mostly a black thing.

The Delta was known for sharecropping from Walls, Mississippi, (which is near Memphis, Tennessee) to Yazoo City, Mississippi. In between these places is where you got the blues. You could see people working and you could hear them singing the blues for miles. Out of each mouth, a new blues tune arrived; some used those tunes to make fortunes. Out of long years of waiting and working, the people always knew there was a brighter day ahead.

Tunica County was the poorest county in the United States. There were other counties that were in need, but some places were considered the "Poorhouse"—a southern term. The town of Tunica was built in the 1800s. Before Tunica was built, Austin was the county headquarters. The first high school was built in Tunica in 1952. The students went two months in the summer and the rest of the time late fall until early spring. Churches have always been plentiful in the Delta. Sunday took care of everything that happened the week before. On Sunday, you had a lot of good things to look forward to: Sunday's dinner, weddings, family gatherings, singing in the choir. Some received the joy of taking the preacher home with them on Sunday.

Let me add that some blacks and whites had their own land in Tunica County and in all of the other counties in the Delta.

Success has come to the Delta, and I can't count the ways. I'll try to name a few: education is better, housing is better, living conditions are better, jobs, health and welfare, and so many other things have happened for the better. The cotton, corn, wheat, rice, barley, fish farms, cattle farms, hunting, trapping, hogs, chickens, and vegetable farms—these were some of the things that kept the Delta alive. Please come with me on the inside of this book.

New workplaces have come to the Delta, and boy, is that good! All across the Delta, people are working and living like people do in any other place in the country. The casinos have become the cornerstones of Tunica County. These places have given jobs to many people far and near. It has something there everybody can do.

Here—where Highway 304 crosses old Highway 61—was a little town called Robinsonville. It had eight stores, one post office, two doctor's offices, and one church close to the town. There was also a grocery store where people came and took up groceries during the week, and where they came on Saturday and Saturday night to have a good time. There would be so many people, you could not walk because of cars. There were night houses or cafes where they went to dance and drink, eat fish sandwiches, or just for plain ole getting down. All of this went out in the late 1950s. People started going north finding a better life. Work was plentiful there, so little by little, most people left. The town of Robinsonville went down. The grocery store where the farmers came and got their groceries stayed opened and became a giant in Robinsonville! It became The Hollywood. People came from all over the country to eat at The Hollywood. Songs were made about it. There were even movies made in Robinsonville. It had begun to look like an old western town. Movie stars were in Robinsonville, and that was big stuff.

The first casino that came to Tunica was the Splash, and the Splash brought in so many people that others started coming. But they did not all go to Tunica. They stopped in Robinsonville, which is ten miles north of Tunica near Memphis, but it is still in Tunica County. Some families had sold out to the Grand Casino. They had been in that part of the county since back in the 1800s. My husband played there when he was a child on the land of the Grand. Our children played there too. They named a road for my husband and his family—Dunn's Road. Each time we pass it, smiles come forth. Just look to the right when you get to Dunn and Highway 61. Right at the information center you will see an old barn, that's what my husband really loved. He told me many tales about that barn.

The Delta is on the rise, and Tunica County is booming.

Come to Tunica County and visit us. What you need, baby, we got it! We are located at the beginning of the Delta. Highway 61 will bring you close to most of the Delta towns. Like everything else, the best is yet to come.

Tunica has been called the Bay Area. It got this name during the 1960's. In 1960, a real movement came to Tunica. It started at the high school. There were teachers there who beat up a young man. I think that they were trying to kill him, but God stepped in and spared his life and today we are grateful. The young man's family went to the head of the schools, and the school did something about it. They fired the teachers. Valer his aunt asked the superintendent to rehire them, and he did. After this incident, other parents felt like they were not alone. Parents became unafraid whereas before it was a known fact that their children would suffer if they said anything. The schools felt that the people who were not teachers were illiterate. We all know that parents are your best resources when it comes to children. Just to have parents who care are what children want and need.

In this same time frame, we put Tunica on the map. We had Sixty Minutes to come down from CBS Television to do a report on how things were in Tunica. They came and talked about some important things, but they couldn't show and tell everything.

Sugar Ditch was one thing that got everyone's attention. People wanted to know what they meant about Sugar Ditch. We had to tell them it really wasn't sugar. It was simply where sewage ran from the white subdivisions down to where the black people lived. So, you see, it wasn't sugar after all.

When all of this aired on Sixty Minutes, the whole nation found out about Tunica County. After that, people started calling, coming, writing, and just trying to find out what they could do to help. They sent truckloads of food, clothes, and whatever else they thought we needed to Tunica. A lot of people would fly in or ride in just to see what they could do to help.

When they got there they said, "My! My! You are sitting on a gold mine!" They said, "This is Solid Gold, we have never seen this much flat land before." So they went back and told their friends. It was all over the "wire." Big businessmen started coming to Tunica. We started having town hall meetings. I said, "I am about to see my dream come true."

When I was in high school, every Friday in civics class we had to say quotations. I loved this one: "I tremble for my country when I reflect that God is just, knowing that His justice won't sleep forever." I think President Abraham Lincoln said that. "Oh! My brother would get off in his quiet kind of way." He would say, "Mildred, I'm going to tell Mom that you say the same thing every Friday. You don't have to try and talk so proper." He didn't mean correct. He meant—I sounded like the people who left the South and went North. When they came back, we could hardly understand anything they said. He would tell my mama (that's what I called her) when he got home each Friday. And she would say to me, "Mildred stop talking so proper." I really don't think she cared. She just wanted to satisfy him. But you know, as I hear people say now, "Whenever I am the MC, I try to get a little preaching in." That's what I was trying to do back then—slipping a little preaching in. I am still preaching today, the only difference is I don't have to slip and do it. Would you believe that people are still trying to make me stop? I smile today just like I smiled when my brother told my mama. I feel like they are just like him— sweet and not meaning any harm.

The Delta has brought a lot of good out of many people. We've always had the blues, but we stacked our problems on top of each other. We stepped on top of them and reached higher. The people here have always been able to take care of themselves. They have raised their own food, made medicine, and made their own clothes. When their babies were born, some ladies assisted with the birth of the babies. Those ladies were called midwives, and they were very much needed. There were only five doctors within about every one hundred miles. The medicine people made themselves was about as good as the doctors. I will name just a few kind of medicines: Root—this is where they would dig up a plant from the earth, cut the roots off, boiled, and put cooking oil in it. They put it on a burn, and it healed. I can't name the plants. For a cold, they cooked the beef and used the oil that was left to rub over their chest. For a high temperature, they used large leaves from a plant and covered the body until the temperatures went down. If a child had pinkeye, they would find a lady with a young baby and she would put breast milk into the eye. For the whooping cough, they would get a frog and hang it over the door until the cough would leave the child and go into the frog. For a cut or bruise, they would put black smut on it from the stovepipe.

If people had to live like that today, too much stress would enter their bodies and minds. Our bodies have become too weak. We could not use that kind of medicine today; if we did, we just might die.

They made corn whiskey too, but I don't know how they made it. They went into the forest (we said the woods) and took all their stuff. Working day and night they made a lot of money. Robinsonville, Mississippi, was the corn whiskey capital of the world. People came from near and far and bought it by the barrels. The law did not permit the sale of homemade corn whiskey; sometimes they would catch the makers, but that just made them go farther into the woods. It also made them work more at night. All of the corn whiskey kingpins drove big, long cars, then like now they looked g-o-o-d. People also made beer and wine at home, and oh, yes, they made something else called homebrew. They said you could get high off of that. I know how to make homebrew. You see, in the Delta when you got the blues, you didn't just sit around, you got up and got busy. Not only in Robinsonville did they do this, but all through the Delta. Everybody, of course, didn't do the same thing, but everybody did something.

I Am the Delta

I was born and reared in Tunica County in Robinsonville, Mississippi, and I lived there until I was seventeen years old.

I went to elementary school at Bowdre Elementary. That's two miles south of Robinsonville. On Sunday the building was Christian Spring Church, but through the week it was Bowdre Elementary. I started there in the first grade. Well, I was supposed to have been in the first grade—that was my first year at school—but I knew how to read when I got there, so my cousin put me in the second grade with her and my twin brothers Robert and S.T. That's where I stayed the whole year. The teacher didn't care as long as you could read.

I walked to school with my brothers, sisters, cousins, and friends. We had to walk about three miles even if it were raining, snowing or sleeting. We had to go; our big sister, Beulah, was one of the teachers. I used to love to go with her on Saturday to the teachers' meeting. That was the day she got paid. Sometimes, I was the only child there. I went to Bowdre until I was in the eighth grade, then I graduated. I had such a good time there especially when we had plays at the end of every year. We also had box suppers. Everybody went to school and took their boxes. The girls would take the food and the boys would bid on the boxes and the one that had the most money would get the box.

I liked spring most of all because I like to walk home in the afternoons with the breeze blowing on my face. My dad and others had begun to break up the land—oooh—the freshness of the earth, the flowers had begun to bud and that sweet aroma would fill the air. It made you glad winter had gone. They would plant the cotton. A few weeks later, we were chopping cotton.

1974

Rev. Dunn, my husband

My first car, 65 Fairlane Ford
My sister Irene sits on the ground.

Bowdre along Highway 61—the place where I was born
and lived until I was eighteen years old

Silos are towers in which feed, either ensilarge or
green fodder, is stored for cattle.

Bowdre Elementary School—Christian Spring MB Church.
My grandmother was a member here. My grandmother, my
mom, and my dad are resting here. Also, other family
members.

The New School
I would love to work here at least one day;
these are the grounds where I played as a child.

We would go to school two months in the summer, and seven months in the winter. When I say we, I mean my fourteen sisters and brothers and myself. After I graduated from Bowdre Elementary School. I went to Tunica County Vocational High School from 1952 until 1956. It is now called Rosa Fort. My brothers and I went—S.T., Robert, Henry, Louis, and Austin, my baby brother. (Henry is deceased.) I was one of the first four-year graduates of that school. S.T. and I. During my high-school days, like any other kid, I really wasn't crazy about school, but I knew I had to have an education to make it in this world. So, I did what I had to do. Sometimes I thought I wasn't learning anything but I stayed there. The teachers didn't teach like I wanted them to, but they taught. I always thought that the teacher should teach what you needed to know and test you on that, not test you on what they thought you knew. Some teachers found out that you didn't know, and they said stuff like, "You are in the ninth grade and you don't know that?" That's what you call putting a student down. Teachers, please stop playing and teach. I heard that is still happening. The child you leave behind might be your doctor, lawyer, or maybe like one of my second-grade students—now he is a principal.

After high school, I went to college, Coahoma Junior, for two years. After that I stayed out of school for a year and found out I couldn't make it without a college education. I had jobs that paid twelve dollars a week in Memphis. I told one owner that I just couldn't make it on twelve dollars a week. I asked if I could work day and night; that would have been sixteen hours a day. He asked me, "Mildred, why do you need so much money?" I told him I had been to college two years and I wanted to go back. He told me that it would be too hard for me to work double, but he would start paying me twenty-five dollars just for asking. But when the cook found out about it, she told his wife and his wife fired me. When he found out about it, he hired me back. By then I knew it was time to go, and I did. The next week I found another job paying nineteen dollars a week, plus tips; I kept it for the rest of the year. I saved enough money to go back to college.

This time I went a long way from home. I went to Alcorn State University, and I really enjoyed those two years. The people were friendly, well, the boys and men anyway. Those years at Alcorn really helped me get my life together. I call them the blessed years. There, under the giant trees is where I heard the voice of God and a friend of mine, call my name. I received my Bachelor's Degree in Education. I started teaching in Memphis, and now I did just that—retired; I got tired of the house and went back to work.

Teaching has been wonderful these forty years. I have taught in the same system. The students have been wonderful. They afforded a good life for me just being around them. It is really hard for me to leave them. Sometimes tears come to my eyes when I think about leaving. My sons say I must come home. I went and couldn't stay.

I was married to the Reverend J. Dunn (who is now deceased) for twenty-eight years. He was a lovely husband and really taught me a lot. There wasn't anything that I would not do for him. I learned to play the piano so I could play for his church choir. We worked as a team. He preached only one sermon that I didn't want to hear. It was entitled "What in Hell Do You Want?" He just didn't say it right. I don't know what the members thought about that sermon.

We have two sons, TyJuan Wells-Dunn and Jarvis DeVor Dunn. TyJuan is the older son. He was born in 1976. He is my firstborn, and my brother-in-law calls him the "Six-Million-Dollar Man." He is now in LeMoyne Owen College and is ready to graduate. He keeps me straight around the house. Jarvis, my second son, was born in 1977. My brother calls him "Man" because he always treated Ty as if he were the baby. Jarvis is a junior at LeMoyne Owen College I am speaking for my husband and myself—they are sweet and obedient young men. I thank God for them.

I started pastoring my husband's church thirteen years ago, and I am still there. Some people say that I am doing too many things and that I should retire, but I haven't yet. First, I was an elder; now I am a bishop pastoring Mt. Ever's Cathedral COGIC in Memphis.

So you see, being from the Delta didn't stop me from doing anything I wanted to do, but, I still get the blues sometimes.

I am from a county that at one time had thirty-seven millionaires. Thirty-six were white, and one was black. The rest of us lived by trial and error, but we made it. Sometimes things would get so tough you got the blues—but you made it. Today, this is the way we live; you can't be sure of anything, but don't give up the will to try.

I am coming close to retiring. I am still enjoying my job that I have had for forty years. I love the sound of the kids chattering in hallways—occasionally one will come in to say "hello" or wave; some even come in and stay with me for a while. I enjoy seeing them learn to read. Most students get in trouble, because they are probably slow in their subject area and can't focus on whatever is going on in the classroom. Those children are still angels and they know it. I treat them as if they have just stepped out of heaven for the first time.

The view from my office is perfect. I am overlooking Southland Mall, on Elvis Presley Blvd. and a large church sits in front of the school, and the large maple trees are beautiful. A lot of times I have to hold back the tears, because I never thought anyone would be this nice to me. I just want the world to know I have a nice principal. His name is mentioned for making a difference in my life.

Looking back over my life, if I had to do it again, I would do it exactly the same way. I would be born in the Delta to my parents Henry and Sallie Wells, as one of fifteen children—six boys and nine girls. My parents were from Holly Springs, Red Banks, Victoria, and those places in the hills. They moved to the Delta before they got married. Mom was the daughter of Bishop E. Cottrell and Mattie Yarbrough-Cottrell, and my dad was the son of Walter Wells and Annie Cochran-Wells. I would do the same things, meet the same people, marry the same man, be the mother of the same sons. I would even be centerfold for *Jet Magazine* again.

Now I want my own TV show. I want to lose sixty pounds. I want to bridge the gap between the home, school, church, and community. I know it can be done, with all of us working together. Our children can live a better life. Our men and women can do the same from the Pacific to the Atlantic, from the Gulf to the North Pole.

Mr. Willis Neely, my principal

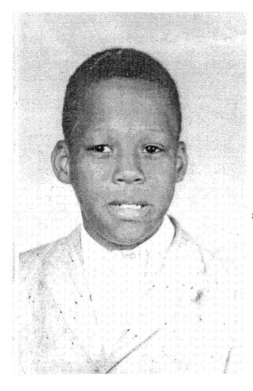

Willis Neely, my
second-grade student

Mrs. Edna Ammons took this picture while visiting with
us. She was my high-school principal's wife.

Jarvis, graduating from Whitehaven High School, and Mom

Jarvis, graduating from Middle School at Havenview

Rev. J. D. Dunn,
my husband

TyJuan Wells Dunn

TyJuan graduated from Whitehaven High School. He went on to get a Bachelor's Degree in Computer Science from LeMoyne-Owen College, Memphis, Tenn.

He is now attending the University of Memphis, working on a Master's Degree in Math.

During high school, he sang in the choir, first tenor, and he was a member of the Computer Science Club and a member of the ROTC Squad.

Good luck, Ty.

—Mom

Jarvis DeVor Dunn

Jarvis graduated from Whitehaven High School. During his high-school year, he attended the Children's Theatre of Memphis. He had leading roles in many plays. The one I loved best was *I Never Saw Another Butterfly*. He plans on pursuing his acting career. He is working on a B.S. in Art at LeMoyne-Owen College, Memphis, Tenn.

Good luck, Jar.

—Mom

Ty is standing
Jarvis (Jar) is kneeling

Mt. Ever's Cathedral
COGIC where I pastor.

"We can bridge these gaps"—I fell so in love with this saying that I shared it with people like presidents and governors. Schools took it and used it, and they didn't get my permission nor did they give me any credit for it. I am not bitter at anyone, because I know life is fair. We have to step up to the home plate, take a stand, hit the ball, and make a home run. No one else can do it for us. In time, I know justice will prevail.

Looking back over the life of man, taking the bitter with the sweet, I can see how we advanced so fast and became educated. We had open minds; we thought a lot; we read a lot; and that became easy for us to do. We had to come up with ways to change. Nothing had been done in so many walks of life, so each day was another milestone back then, and now. We still must keep focus. It does not matter whether we are in the Mississippi Delta or upstate New York. Whatever it was that was needed, you figured a way to do it. If you needed cornbread and didn't have corn meal, you made meal by mixing flour and grits; if it was food or clothes you needed and you didn't have money, you gave a day's work; if it were lipstick you need and didn't have it, you used red crepe paper; if you wanted straight hair, you pulled a hot comb through it; if you wanted your patent leather shoes to shine, you put oil on them or a hot biscuit.

In the words of a famous man, "You figured it out." This is what all of us must do to be productive. Do not wait for others to bring you an idea, because sometimes your way of thinking could be the jackpot. It is okay to listen to others, but don't make that your master. Too many of us are searching for something that we already have. Just use what you have to the fullest.

I have always thought I could do anything I wanted to do, and for many years it has come true. Cooking, washing, sewing, cutting the yard, cleaning the house, fixing hair, playing the piano, writing songs, singing, preaching, building houses and churches. People always told me I could do anything that I wanted to do. Just one and only one person told me I couldn't do something, and this lady taught school. She said to me, "Mildred, you can't marry my son." Well, she told me why—she said, "You see, you live on a plantation, and I am a school teacher, and therefore, I don't want you to marry my son." I was only thirteen years old and wasn't thinking about getting married. My biggest hope was that her son did not think like his mother. After all he was his mother's child. My hope came true, because he was ashamed to hear his mother say that to me. She put me down low.

As the years passed on, I went to high school and then to junior college. After junior college, I went to Alcorn University. During my last year at Alcorn University, just before graduation, I came home, and my mom told me that the same teacher that had put me down wanted to see me. So I went to the Bowdre Elementary School where she was still teaching. I was glad to see her, and I believe she was glad to see me. We talked for a while and went back to yesteryears—oh, I must have been seven or eight years old when she came there. By now, her son was living in Chicago, Illinois. She said, "Mildred, my son wants you to write to him, here is his address." Let us figure out what made her change her mind . . . We have to be careful about what we say to our children, because we really don't know who they are. As one of my sisters always says: "Don't mess with a child. Treat them all well because you don't know who he or she might be." This is the way things happened in the Delta. Most of the people were on the same level, but some thought that they were better than others. After I grew up, I really felt sorry for the lady and her son. Both passed away at early ages in their—I believe fifties.

I believe if you struggled and made it through the Delta's life, you can do anything. Yesterday, I went to the Board of Education for Memphis City Schools. I threw my hat in the ring for Superintendent of Memphis City Schools. If anyone can do it, I can. My reason for believing I would make a good Superintendent of Memphis City Schools is because they took the program I wrote and used it. That was "Bridging the Gap Between the Home, School, Church, and Community." I think I could do a better job with my own program than anyone else can. I was also told I was a fool to let them see it. I didn't think I was a fool. I was trying to get a grant to help within the community. I keep thinking about a car the dealer let me test drive. I could not keep it, because it wasn't mine. At that time I could not say much. But now the Lord has made me strong, and I am going to face them with facts. Pray I am blessed. The Delta taught me a lot: how to be strong, face facts, treat people right, stay prayerful, and know, with God on your side, you can't fail.

Family

My parents were from Marshall County, Holly Springs, Mississippi. My father was Henry Wells II. His father was Henry Wells I. He was a descendent of Ida B. Wells; his mother was the late Ms. Annie Cockran of Louisiana. They moved to Holly Springs at a young age. Walter Henry Wells and Annie were married, and to this union, five children were born—my dad, Henry; his brothers Frank "Joe" and El; and his sisters Priscilla and Chankum. My dad grew up and moved to White Station, Tennessee, and lived there for a few years. Later he decided to visit an older sister who lived in Dubbs, Mississippi. That's when he met my mom. My dad was educated in Marshall County, Holly Springs, Mississippi. He had the name Cool Touch; I think that was because he danced so cool. He called me Bill. He said to me one day, "Bill, when I was dancing, we did a dance called 'Getting Low As a Toe' and I could really do it," and I said, "Papa, I bet you could."

My mother was Sallie Yarbrough Cottrell. Her dad was Bishop Elijah Cottrell—the seventh Bishop of the CME Methodist Church. Her mother was Mattie Yarbrough. My mother had two sisters and one brother—Mary Lee Kizer, Lee Ethel, and James Hamilton. She was educated in Holly Springs. She finished high school and went to MI College. She later moved to Dubbs with her uncle, the elder Isaiah Bell, who was married to my dad's sister, who was Cora. That is when my mom and dad met and later got married. After a while they had fifteen children—and were living in Robinsonville. There my parents farmed. My mom worked for the government in the 1930s, teaching people to cook, sew, can foods, and showing them how to become homemakers.

My brothers are Collins "Jake," Robert, S.T., Henry III (deceased), Louis, and Austin. My sisters are Iowan (deceased),

Beulah, Mattie, Cora, Irene, Flora "Sis" Barbara (deceased), and Ernestine. I enjoy being part of a big family. It has taught me the value of love, respect, friendship, the church, and the Lord's people. All of my brothers and sisters are married with families and everyone lives in Memphis, Tennessee, except two. My sister Beulah White lives in Tunica, Mississippi, and Flora "Sis", lives in Oakland, California. Everyone is still working. We retire but, then, land another job. I went back to the same job, and I am enjoying it better the second time around.

Our parents taught all of us to do the best we can, no matter what job we take. We were taught that it is an honor to have any job. I started to work when I was six years old. All of us started by the time we were six years old. It really didn't hurt, and it gave us self-control and self-discipline. We could not chop cotton at six years old, but we could pick cotton, wash dishes, feed the chickens and ducks, watch the baby, comb our mom's hair after dinner, etc.

In the evening after everyone got home, we padded the quilt with cotton. Everyone could do that, and when we finished the padding of the quilt, the elder siblings would tack the top to the bottom. The top of the quilt was pieced together from scraps of materials that were left over from the clothes that were made by Mom and my big sisters. Each quilt had a name: Star, Monkey Wrench, H, Tuff Boy, Britches, the Sun, the Moon, and many others. After the top was tacked to the bottom, we put it on the frames. The frame was two long wood poles, one placed on each side of it. When the quilt was placed on the frames, we tied four long ropes that we had hung from the top of the house to each end of it. We then could raise and lower the quilt as needed so that we could work on the quilt. When it was let down low enough, we could sit in chairs and sew it together. We would reach as far as we could sew a section of it, then we would roll that side of the quilt up so that we could reach another section of it. Sometimes other grown-ups would come and visit. They would sit around sewing on the quilt laughing and talking. It was kind of like having a party. Sometimes they would go from house to house sharing in the quilting.

Everybody would share in the chores year in and year out. We went to school and church, played, and did things that other children did. Most people did mostly the same thing.

At night, we used to sit on the porch in Robinsonville and look at the lights of Memphis. Last night, I was driving along Shelby Drive and saw the lights in Robinsonville. My! Things have really changed. When I was growing up in Robinsonville, at night everything was dark. We didn't have all of the bright lights from the casinos. But now, everything has changed. You can see the lights from the casinos from miles and miles away.

Mr. William Henry Wells
My dad

Mrs. Sallie Wells
My mom

Front Row
Collins, Robert
Back Row
Austin, Henry Jr., Carl and S.T.
My Brothers

Papa

Mrs. Mattie Malone was my grandmamma. Her famous words were, "It's a mean ole wind that don't never change."

Cousin Ida Thompson

Aunt Mary Lee Middlebrook
My mom's sister and Ida's mom

Mrs. Flora Wells London

This is my sister, who always said she was going out west, and she did. I remember when she used to stand and watch the sun set, and she would say, "Bright sun, here I come." I'm not sure what it was about the west that was so enchanting. Most people in (Tunica) or R.V., Mississippi, went north. Not this young lady. I guess something was telling her, "Go west, young lady, go west." She has been there for a number of years. All of her five children grew up there—and her grandchildren. California is surely Golden West Country.

left to right
Collins, Irene, Beulah, Mattie, Robert, Mildred, Ernest
back row
Carl, Cora, Austin, and S.T.
My sisters and brothers and me

Percy Golden, Celestine's older son.

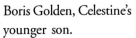

Boris Golden, Celestine's younger son.

Collins' grandsons

Mrs. Mary Wells, Collins'
lovely wife.

Mr. Collins Wells and his two beautiful daughters
Celestine Golden and Erma Jean Lowe

Mrs. Stephana, Drew and Angel Sander
This is the daughter and grandchildren of S.T. and Helen.

Darren, Evetta,
"Rena" & Amyah
My brother Robert's
children

Amyah, Robert's granddaughter

Delta Cotton Fields

The people of the Delta lived amazing lives. Originally there were woods and trees for miles around. People started moving in from other states, cutting down trees and building small houses; this was right after slavery. The government owned that land. After slavery, they would give the black man forty acres of land and two mules. Some of the blacks accepted the land and the mules, and some did not. The ones who accepted the land would clear the land of trees and plant cotton, corn, vegetable gardens, raise cattle, hogs, chicken, and whatever they could. This was the way of life for these blacks. There were other blacks that wouldn't accept the land, or maybe they just didn't receive any. Those were the ones who lived with the white sharecroppers. Those whites rented land from the government, started a farm, and allowed the blacks to live on their farms, and this went on until about the early 1970s.

This was a way of life for a lot of people in the Delta. Each farm had a grocery and one or two churches for the people. There were many houses on a plantation. One might have red houses, another brown, gray, but not many white houses. If you lived in a white house you were considered a "big shot". If you know what I mean. The blacks living on a plantation didn't have any money. They barely received four hundred dollars a year. In the plantation on which they lived, the owner or boss, as this man was often called, would get the doctor if anyone got sick. He also made sure they had food through winter and he got the people out of jail. In those days, blacks in the Delta could not drink a Coke because the people in the stores would not sell Cokes to blacks. They had to drink fruit drinks. This was one step above slavery. Most of the people's education was about the same, blacks and whites. The whites did have schools and school buses, and what they learned the blacks learned through the black women worked at the white people's houses. These women listened to what the white people learned and came home and taught it to their families. These are the kinds of things that went on throughout most of the Delta.

People were kind of lost in the Delta. They were not keeping the kind of records that they should. That's when the counties came about, so that they could keep up with the people better. Jackson, Mississippi became the headquarters. When babies were born, they would have to record the birth and send those records to Jackson. They were blessed to have the midwives to deliver the babies, because there were not many doctors around. Sometimes their parents would name them one thing, and it would come back another, because the midwives spelled the names incorrectly. There were people who having grown, then found out that they were using one name, while their birth certificates, had another name. But they did well to get the babies there. As time went on, it got better and better. People were too busy planning for the family and making a better life.

This is one of the counties that I'll share with you. This is where I lived, Tunica County. In this county there were many plantations. The white farmers would rent land from the government, start a farm, and then have the blacks come over and live on their rented land. This land was called "Mary Mack Land." The blacks that lived on this land were called sharecroppers. They would chop and pick the cotton, and at the end of the year, the farmers would give them a little money. They said they were taking the food, rent, and doctor's bills out of the money given. Sometimes the plantation owner might give them two hundred or three hundred dollars for a whole year's work. They would stay in the owner's debt, because they would have to borrow the rest of the year from him. When the year had come to an end, most of the people would run away in the night. Because they were still under a form of slavery. At night, the plantation owners would get other blacks to crawl under houses, sit beside the fireplace underneath the house, and listen to what was being said in the house. If they heard the people talking about running away, they would go back and tell the plantation owner, and he would not let those people have any money. Sometimes, it didn't matter because some of their kinfolks would come down from the north, and the blacks would catch a ride back to Chicago or Detroit. The next morning, children would wake up and find their playmates gone. That gave them a sad feeling.

The biggest hurt we ever had was when a little girl's father came down from some place in the north and stole his daughter from her grandmother. We kept waiting and waiting for her to come back, and about eight years later, she did. She was about seventeen years old when she returned. She had changed. She had taken on the city ways. Her father was in jail. She had been in a home for girls. Oh, we didn't care. We were just glad to see her. For a while, she appeared to be the same, but a young man spotted her because she was looking cute and he took her hand in marriage. We thought they were wrong for each other, but they did okay. On the day of Martin Luther King's death, the world went mad. Her husband was in one of the riots in Detroit and got killed. To us, it was like having our playmate taken again. He was a pretty good ole guy. He went to church with us. His uncle was one of the preachers in the church. This was Delta life.

The Delta Cotton Fields were what people looked forward to for six days. My sister reminded me, last night, on how it was when she came along. She said, "Girl . . . when I first started picking cotton, they were only paying sixty-five cents a day." Then she said, "Honey, you got paid well at $1.95 a day." I told her that the five cents they took out were supposed to have gone to the IRS. But guess what? They never saw it. She said, "How do you know?" I told her the IRS could only track me back to when I started to work in Memphis, Tennessee.

Some people don't want to take a lot, just a little bit. Some people are really that way. I remember this lady and I went to work together every day, and in the mornings, she would stop and go into every room we passed by and get just a little something from each one   . She would get a broken piece of chalk, two or three sheets of paper, broken or short pencils—anything that she could take, she would. She didn't need to take anything, but she did. She would say to me, "You had better learn how to do this, if you want to make it in life." I told her that to take anything is wrong. It does not matter how small or how large; wrong is wrong. That's why when grown-ups tell children to do wrong and they do it, I get upset with the children. I always tell the children when they see an adult doing wrong to get away from them and tell somebody. I get upset with the grown-ups, too, but it is hard for them to change. Catch the child while he or she is young.

In the Delta we were taught common sense. Most of the teachers had the Delta Cotton Field mother wit. They taught from the Bible, old newspapers, comic books, catalogs, and old books with the backs off of them. You never knew the name of the books; you just learned to read them. Teachers knew nothing about manuals. They did the best with what they had. The Delta Cotton Field teachers did better than the teachers now. These teachers have Master's Degrees, Bachelor's Degrees, forty-five hours above a Master's Degree, and PhDs, and children still can't read. That concerns me a lot, but we are going to bridge that gap. It used to be the other way around; the teachers did not have degrees, and the students knew how to read. Back then we did not know anything about special education, everybody was expected to learn, and we did. We were afraid not to learn. When we went to bed at night we kept learning. We slept with our book under our head, so we could dream about our work. If we didn't know it, we got beaten by the teacher. Early in the morning when the children went to school, the first thing the teacher would have them do was go into the woods and get lots of small sticks (switches), and about lunch time, all of those were gone, because the teacher had broken them on the students. So, they were sent back and got more sticks. At the end of the day, those were gone, but we learned. I guess sometimes the children would try to run, but it did not do any good, because the other students would catch him or her and bring them back to the teacher. I am not putting the teachers down; that was just the way it was. I don't want us to return to those days of beating up students, but I do want us to return to the days of learning, yes. I am glad teachers can't whip children anymore, because a teacher whipped me once for nothing. I think she was just showing off for her son. You remember the one that said she didn't want me to marry her son? She was the one who did it. Maybe the food our children and parents eat now has a lot to do with how we react to certain things, like learning and keeping your children on the right path, etc.

The Mississippi Cotton Field Delta

Tunica County in the 1800's

Tunica County in the 1800s—people lived close to the river. They hunted, fished, and raised hogs, cattle, and chickens. They lived on plantations. Not many could read—black or white—but they all worked together for the common cause. They worked all week and went to church on Sunday. The preachers gave them the Word. Religion played a major role in the Delta, because people would be working in the fields and be moved by the spirit. The people would sing spirituals or blues. It was the hard times that kept them humming all the time. Daddies smoked pipes and mothers pulled the babies on the cotton sack. This went on until the sun went down. They built cotton gins to clean and clear the cotton of seeds and life went on.

During the 1800s, there was not a town called Tunica. The county site was a little town called Austin. This is where all the information was kept. Trains, buses, and trucks did not come into the town. Freight was transferred in and out by mules and wagons. Everything that came in came down or up the river. That mighty Mississippi River has been a big business since the beginning of time.

In Mississippi, there was an island in Tunica County called Rabbit Island. This is where the lighthouse was. A gentleman by the name of Fabor Mhoon would get out and light the lantern each night, so that when the boats would pull in, they would be able to see the island. They would bring the freight in on the barge and put it on Mr. Mhoon's wagon. Then, he would take it to Austin, and whatever the people in Austin had ready to be taken out, Mr. Mhoon would bring it back to Rabbit Island and wait to put it on the barge so it could reach its proper destination.

Mr. Mhoon was a black man. He was married and had a family: two sons—I believe their names were Josh and William. The sons also married and had families. One of Mr. Fabor Mhoon's grandsons married my sister, and they had two sons and four daughters. Mhoon's Landing is still there, but I believe Rabbit Island has disappeared. The Mhoons contributed a lot to Tunica County. There were other families who made great contributions to Tunica County and the Delta as a whole, blacks and whites.

When the town of Tunica was built, it had class. We had stepped up from a small place to a town. In the county, there was not a high school for blacks until 1952. There were about two private high schools, one in Tunica and one in Prichard, Mississippi. The students would have to go and stay until the weekend. They came home and got things together like food, get their clothes washed and went back. The elementary schools were held in churches. There were high schools in Clarksdale, Holly Springs, and other places in Mississippi. Memphis, Tennessee, was always close to Tunica County; some children went to school here—and I said "here" because this is where I am doing the writing. Make no mistake, we faced each day with open minds. We were free to wander, explore and create and that's what the people in the Delta did.

In the Delta, parents learned to read along with the children. There were parents who waited for the children to come home daily so they could learn new words. On Sunday they would learn to read by reading the Bible along with the preacher, or some of those parents who could read would read for the preacher. There were not many cars back then. People either walked or rode mules, horses, wagons, and buggies. Their hope was to continue until they could make things better, and glad they had a strong drive for higher self-esteem.

There are many towns in the Delta. May I inform you that there are other states with flat land. Mississippi is not the only one. But it is the one that left an impression on me. There were days we all came together on common ground, both black and white, to support the county of Tunica; but after that, people went their separate ways.

The Delta was just different. Life was supposed to have been hard, and slavery was supposed to have been hard, but people still found happy hours. They had house fun, backyard fun, walking the roads at night, playing games, dancing, singing; even picking cotton at night became a sport. When the moon was bright, people would get their sack, go to the fields, and pick cotton for two to three hours. Unlike daytime, this was fun at night; but when day came, it became work. That proves that anything in this life can be enjoyable; it's just how you look at it.

Big families in Tunica County were common. Some families had ten to fifteen children, and some even had nineteen to twenty. That was the way of life back then. Everybody took care of himself or herself. Children started working at an early age. When they were not working, they were at school or church. There were a few crimes back then. I really don't think people had time to get into much trouble. There was a jail in Tunica County, but people thought too much of themselves to go.

In the Delta, we never gave up. We never went to bed and got up with the same thing on our minds. "You can make it if you try." I looked upon the Delta as a shining star. It gave light to so many, it really made you think. Somebody said we were poor, but we didn't know it. The only thing we knew was we got the blues sometimes, and when we did we would put it into a song and a dance. One thing that people learned in the Delta: there was no quitting time. You went from one thing straight into another, until it was time to go to bed.

In Tunica, about twenty men owned the whole county. There were about nine whites and eleven blacks. The county had many little towns. Some of them had one or two stores. They sold everything in them from food to diamonds. Tunica was very slow to get started, but now we are on a roll. I believe one writer said, "We can't stop now—we are just going to keep on building."

Mr. Fabor Mhoon's Descendents

School Days
1940-41

Leo Mhoon

Leo Mhoon

We call her Lil Rene after her grandmother. She is a sweetie; her real name is Tatia Thompson. She is the mother of two lovely children: Justin and "Putty Mama." Lil Rene is my grandniece.

Justin, really, Mr. Cutie, look at that big smile. He's such a handsome boy. He is in the 5th grade. My great-grand nephew, Lil Rene's son.

McKenzie Caburn

Harry Ellis McMillan Jr. and "Putty Mama"—
McKenzie Coburn

Big Rene grandmother to Ellis
great-grandmother to McKenzie

Walter Baker

Robinsonville In The Older Days Delta Town

Now We Reach All Counties

Being born and growing up on a plantation in this now-great country town, I will start from the beginning from a family of fifteen children, a mother and a father, cousins, aunts, uncles, grandmothers, grandfathers—so many times we stared at the horizon. It was like being lost in a fountain searching for happiness. The more I searched, the more I found. Church first, school second, then I advanced out into the things around me. May I bring my readers closer to home? I want my readers to feel what I felt and to see what I saw. More than that, I want you to relive this life with me as I travel down this path.

In the 1900s, my daddy and mom moved to Tunica, Mississippi—by way of Holly Springs, Mississippi. Tunica is the county seat. They lived on a small plantation farm called Dubbs. Finally, they moved closer to Memphis, Tennessee. They moved to Robinsonville, Mississippi. This became home for us. Where most of the children were born on a plantation. We went to a church school. Of course, those were the only schools we had, church schools and home schools.

Robinsonville was a weekend town. People did not show up much during the week. Everyone had to work in the fields. Sometimes during the week, they might get a chance to go to town. I remember one day my mom and I went to Robinsonville; no one was in town but us. She bought whatever she went to get, then she decided to give me a dime and told me to go and buy some ice cream, and I did. After buying the ice cream, I had a nickel left. I decided to put that nickel in the slot machine. I really wasn't expecting to win anything; I just wanted to do something with that nickel. Out of the slot machine came all of this money. I turned and started running but the lady in the store said, "No, baby, that is your money; wait and let me put it in a bag." She gave it to me, and I was afraid to take it to my mom. But there wasn't anyone else to give it to. If I had seen someone else to give the money to before I got to my mom, I think I would have given it to them. When I got back around the street where my mom was, I tried to make an excuse. I said, "Mom, I messed around and put a nickel in the slot [like I didn't know what I was doing, but I did know what I was doing all along; I was trying to win some money] and this is what came out." I showed her the money, and she said, "Girl, give me that money!" We went home and counted it. Guess what? It was three dollars. That was big money back then. I was so glad of that money.

I came home, went on the Fish Lake, and started fishing—oh, there were only a few crawfishes and perches in that small lake, but boy, too much garlic. That afternoon, something terrible happened to me. I went running to papa, and he said, "gal, get away"—then I ran to my sister, and she started running away from me. I flew to my mama, and she said, "Oh, Lord, my child—and what is wrong?" The only thing I could do was cry. After crying, I was okay—I know someone will figure out what happened.

I am full-grown now, guess what? The slots are back in Robinsonville big-time, casinos, casinos, and more casinos. I don't want to go, but people are there from all over the world. Day and night the highways stay full of cars. Years ago we had one highway, later we got another one, old Highway 61 and new Highway 61. I can't count the expressways we have now. One expressway is coming across the country all the way into Robinsonville. We never thought Robinsonville would get famous, but it has. One of my little nieces—well, my first niece—used to sing a song and it went this way:

"Here is a little girl from Robinsonville, let's see what she can do, she can do the pony—ya—the pony—ya—the pony— ya—she can do the pony—ya and then she'll ride away."

She was smart then, and she is still smart today. She is married and has two sons, and grandchildren. What hurts me is the fact that the girl looks like a teenager, and I know I'm only eight years older than this young lady. She gets her rest. I think the mailman thought her husband was her dad. It's all good—her husband is a sweet man, like mine was; he allowed her to get a lot of rest. I love my other nieces and nephews, but you know, she is the queen because she was first. The first niece of the family is the queen, so we named her Queen Esther Washington Edward.

In the old days, we had to be the movie stars; we did our dances and sang our songs, but now they have the real thing. Every time you turn on the TV or ride down the road, you hear or see real big movie stars, big talk-show hosts, golf club tournaments, race tracks, boxing, and circuses—just name whatever you want, it's there. The only difference I see in Robinsonville and Las Vegas is you can walk to Robinsonville and you have to ride to Las Vegas. The town people can leave the cotton fields and walk straight to the casinos. Money or not, you can go to the casinos. Now, that might not be a good idea to go straight to the casinos from work with all of your money. But we, Delta people, have given a lot to the casinos. After working a lifetime for free, we were ready for real jobs. Not only do we have the Delta Blues, I think by now the whole world has the Delta Blues; from what I hear, all roads lead to the casinos, especially in this little Delta Town, Robinsonville, Mississippi—Tunica County.

Queen Ester

It's Time For Me To Relive

Plantation life was the way of life for black folk back then with the exception of those who owned their own land. There were some black families at Robinsonville who owned land there and some still do.

The plantation life was not a bad life if you didn't know any other life. You worked on the farm picking and chopping cotton; you planted your own garden and truck patches. That was the big garden where everything was planted. The house garden was planted close to the house, so you could run out and get what you needed instead of going to the store.

There were people living in different plantations, maybe 100-150 families. All families did about the same thing. They went to church on Sunday. But it was Saturdays that they lived for. The children went to school during the week. We had seven months of school. Two months in the summer, and five in the winter. During the elementary years, children walked four to five miles to school, rain or shine. Most schools went to sixth grade, and some went to the eighth grade. For many years, people living on the plantation didn't go to high school, but they were not illiterate. They knew what they needed to know for that time and period. They worked religiously and led a good life for themselves and their families.

This part of the country is called the Delta, meaning flat land. You can see miles and miles; the beauty of the Delta's life was you didn't need a telephone. You could walk out the door, see what everybody was doing, and find out who was at home. Back in those days, people didn't drive cars; they rode mules and horses, and the buggy was the real deal. If you had a little money, you bought a horse and buggy and rode to church on Sunday or wherever you wanted to go. Some people had mules and wagons.

The dresses ladies wore on the plantation were fancy. Most people made their clothes, men and women. The ladies who knew how to press and curl hair did so. On Friday night and Saturday, people would go to a certain house on the plantation and get their hair fixed. There were men who did the hair cutting. The men went from house to house getting their hair cut for the weekend. The next week, the same things started all over again. Monday morning started early, with milking the cows, feeding the hogs, feeding ducks and chickens, and going to the fields. People rushed to get to the fields to do work. It was work, but it was also a form of socializing. The day ended at 6:00 PM for the women, and the day ended at 7:30-8:00 PM for the men. Men and women did the same kind of farm work, with one exception: the men plowed the fields. The children in those days worked right along beside the parents in the fields. That was the reason they went to split section schools. As time went on, people became more educated in their own minds; then, they started to look for a different life.

The wars made a big difference in the lifestyles of most people. But World War I and World War II were completely different wars. Men got a chance to leave the Delta Cotton Fields and saw the world had another side. World War I veterans went away and fought in the war, but when they came back, things were the same. Now that was blue as blue could be. World War II made the big difference. Men left the Delta and went to the army. They came back home looking good. Those uniforms were neat, with shiny shoes, caps, belts, hair cut neatly—and you could tell they felt good about themselves, from the way they walked. A lot of guys married girls they never would have married if they hadn't gone to war. Some of the men could not read or write before they left the Delta. When they left and stayed away for a while, they wanted to hear from home. So, they got busy and learned to read and write, because some of the soldiers found out that their pals were writing to their girlfriends. They had a reason to learn to read and write.

My big brother went to World War II, and he is still reliving his experiences. He tells me all the time what he did, where he went—and for the time that I am listening, I am in all of those places with him. He talks about the South Pacific; he was located somewhere in the Philippines—well, I guess it was New Guinea, because he loved that place. He said if he had his wish and could go any place he wanted, he would go back to Milne Bay, Papua New Guinea. When he was away in the army, he showed all of us just how much he really loved us. He used to send us so much stuff: pillows, watches, rings—you name it. One thing that I can remember well was when he sent home a big box of chewing gum; boy, we had a ball chewing gum. Our mama or big sisters would hide it, and we could find it. I believe that was the sweetest gum I have ever tasted. He loves to tell us about how he sent money home, and my mom spent it all on my big sisters, keeping them beautiful. And that is the truth.

Those girls used to go to Memphis and buy fur coats, feather hats, high-heeled shoes—you name it. The only thing I would say, I'd be glad when I get to be a big girl so that I can dress like my big sisters. He treated all of us well, and even today, he and his wife would give not only to family members, but anyone who is in need. He is eighty-three years old, and I can tell you that he's still young, because he works everyday and drives where he wants to go; he is a big deacon at his church in Memphis, Tennessee. He tells everybody that "work" is good for you, it keeps you alive and keeps your mind alert. Believe me, I am going to take the guy's word, and I am just going to keep on working. Just yesterday, I received my professional license from the Department of Education saying that I can teach ten more years. Then I can renew the license if I choose to continue teaching. Well, I just might renew again. One big wish I have had all of my days is that everyone could get at least four years of college. It makes you feel good. If you get a degree and don't do anything with it but wash dishes, that's okay if that's what you want to do, fine. One never gets too old to learn. I recall back in the day when I had gone to college only two years; people told me I had enough education. I heard what they said, but did I pay attention? No—because I knew I had to live my own life, so I went back to college.

As I look back, it wasn't hard; I worked day and night. People wanted to give me money, pay my way; but I said no, because I was taught everything came with a price.

In the Delta, parents taught their daughters that they were blooms from the magnolia tree. That meant you were sweet, pretty, nice—just name the good stuff, and you named the girls of the Delta. They also taught their sons well. My thinking now is that they thought if girls stayed in their places, boys would be okay. Our parents made us feel good about ourselves. That was one way they could teach the children self-control, they didn't have to follow them around. They made them feel as if they were too good to do anything wrong. That still sticks with you especially when you are full-grown. That is a phrase my brother-in-law used, "full-grown." Parents, it's okay to make your children feel good about themselves. It will be a help to them and you, too. When I was in the second grade (I was never in the first grade), I had this little friend I would go home with for lunch. She would make a jelly sandwich for each of us. We would then say goodbye to her mom and run back to school. Her mom was ill and eventually died. We still went to her house for those jelly sandwiches. The name of that jelly was Rex—hmmm, it was good. We stayed friends through the years. She married one of my cousins. I really didn't like that because I thought she was too young to get married. It didn't work out. She moved to St. Louis. She had this little cousin who used to help us with our lessons. He was a smart guy, kind of mean to us when we would not do what he said. His sister and I used to have to go to the blackboard and write our spelling words, and before the teacher called out the first word, we would turn around looking for him to tell us how to spell it. We did the same thing in math; he would write the answers, and we would copy. He grew up and went north in the 1950s. He married this cute girl.

Another time I like to remember was when I was small chasing butterflies. I loved chasing butterflies; I think I was fascinated by the beautiful colors, yellow, purple, black and orange. Now no matter what I see a child doing, I think that it is cute, because they enjoy what they enjoy. Everything is beautiful when you can see it through the eyes of a child.

My mind goes back again to the tin-top house. When it rained at night, the music—sweet music from the soft raindrops—put you into a heavenly rest. The soft rain also made the dirt smell good enough to eat. Out in the hills where my mom and dad came from, people did eat the dirt, or so I was told. My grandma would go back to the hills, dig into the side of one of those hills, and get some clean red dirt, and they would eat it. But you could not eat that Delta dirt.

The ice cream my cousin and sister made was the best. I wish I could relive that night they made the ice-cream custard. We did not have an ice-cream freezer, so they got an old washtub, broke up the ice, put it in the tub, then poured the custard into a molasses bucket; they put the top on the bucket, then took turns spinning that bucket until the ice cream froze. We stayed up until about four o'clock in the morning, but the ice cream was s-o-o-o good! That was a real Delta party. That was just home folks having a good time. A lot of Delta parties were just like that. Even with grown-ups, a little cutting and shooting, but not much.

This is in the Delta near the Mississippi River.

This is one of the Delta's famous barns.

Mr. Charles Tatum, one of the owners of Tatum Estate in Robinsonville, Mississippi—Just back from Detroit Mich. Home, sweet home.

Truck Patch

Mr. Charles Tatum's lovely home
I have never seen a tree as lovely as a house.

It has been a hard day. It's time to rest. Picking peas is really hard. Charles Tatum and Mildred Wells-Dunn

Mrs. Helen Wells, one of my sister-in-laws
This girl has too much energy.
S.T.'s wife

Delta Tools

An Estate from the 1800's
It belonged to, brother Charlie and sister B

Another historical house

The Church Life

The church life involved going to meetings on Sunday. The ladies dressed in fancy dresses, long puff sleeves, high hats, large purses, and high-heeled shoes; the children wore fancy clothes, too. The big girls mostly wore white dresses to church on Sunday; the boys wore white shirts and short pants. The men wore peg-leg suits and hard hats. When they dressed in that attire, that was the life.

The sisters sat on one side of the church, and the brothers sat on the other. Children were in the middle, so that everyone could keep an eye on them. The deacons always had their place near the rostrum or pulpit where the preacher sat. In those days, women were not allowed in the pulpit. You could walk to the edge and wait for the preacher to come to you for whatever the reason was. Mostly though, the Delta churches were Baptist churches. Now and then you would find a few Church of God in Christ, Methodists, and maybe some others. The Baptist shouted rough. You had to hold them to keep them from hurting themselves. COGICs jumped, danced, and rolled around on the floor. I am a COGIC, but I couldn't do any of the things that the other people were doing because I was too busy trying to find out what they were doing whatever. The Methodist Church back then was a long way off, but now I remember there was a Methodist Church next to a school where we had church. My cousin and I would go out to the outside bathroom, tiptoe over to the church, and stand under the window, and we never heard them say a word. So really, we could not figure out what they were doing inside; we just knew they were quiet.

If there were anything to be found out, my cousin and I were busy trying to find out what it was. She runs my revival every summer. I am the pastor of the church, and she is an evangelist. She travels all over the United States and Canada spreading the gospel. I understand now what the Bible means when it says, "Bring up a child in the way he should go." Even if he strays away, she or he will return.

I know I am back to do the will of Him who called me. It was in 1960 when he called me with that loud voice. I thought everybody heard him, but just one girl heard that voice. She walked all the way upstairs, opened my door, came in, and said to me, "Mildred, I heard someone call you," and I replied I heard it, and I called her name, then she left and went back downstairs. We were at Alcorn University. I wish I could see her now so we could talk about that night—really, we never spoke of it again. My feelings are that we were afraid to discuss it. She had a brother that went to school there. I believe she was COGIC, maybe not. I remember she read her Bible a lot. There was another young lady that I knew, and she was COGIC. She had everything she wanted. Her father was, as we say, a big-time preacher, because one year he brought the message here when the saints came to Memphis town. You had to be with the "in" crowd to do that. That was her father. He and her mother came to the school and picked up their baby. I stood there watching her get into this big blue shining car with her parents. I think I was hoping they would say hello to me, but they never looked my way. I hated to see her go. She was sweet, maybe too sweet. I think people took advantage of her. My thing with that was she seemed like she had everything she wanted, and I was struggling, (now, as I am writing this article, the tears are just rolling down my cheeks.) not knowing where my next meal was coming from. I watched her and her parents until they were out of sight. Her parents were probably so upset they didn't notice me. That taught me to smile, speak, wave my hand, and nod my head or something, when I see people. I believe that was the only time in my life that I felt that way, and I know why. I was a long way from home and felt I saw one of my own. I never knew the parents but I felt close to them because they were COGIC. I felt let down because of the way I had been taught, in this church. I thought all saints were nice, friendly, and holy. They didn't show any of this. I think they were from a big city, down on the Gulf. But times have changed. If my sister and brother in Christ do something strange, I really don't think much about it. I am reminded of the Saturday I went to this church and spoke to the preacher; he spoke and smiled, but he did not know who I was at first. When he found out, he yelled at me and I just moved on. Maybe I should have been upset, but I wasn't, because the reason for the screaming came clearly, yesteryears.

I have always been wrapped up in the church. My husband was a preacher. His family and my family are busy getting the word of God out to His people.

Outside bath room

Church

Delta Hospitality

Delta's southern hospitality is one you don't want to miss! To have been a part of such hospitality still gives me the chills. Some had money, some had soul, some had love, some spirit, but we all had the Lord on our side.

Everyone worked during the week, but on evenings and weekends we all met at a common place—the water hydrant in the evenings, town on Saturday, and church on Sunday.

The men and boys also had a sport they did on Sundays, baseball after church. People met in large groups in a pasture and formed a baseball team. And some of the women and children went to cheer them on as they played. My brothers and my daddy played. That was one of the big-time sports in the Delta in the 1800s, and as the time went on, it got larger and larger. My brother Henry Junior almost got into the big time.

Women played a sport called softball, and something else that was common for relaxation was singing, great singing. People went miles at night to hear these groups. People came from far and near on horseback, walking, wagons, buggies, and any other way that they could. Church revivals brought the same crowd. People came from far and near to church at night.

People shared when one was in trouble. The whole community came forward to help or share into the joy or sadness of our fellowman or person. That kind of life was healing for the body. People had less stress in those days than they have now. They ate mostly healthy foods, because the garden gave them all kinds of fresh vegetables. There were fresh fruits and whatever one needed to live a healthy life. The homes were full of hospitality. Families visited from house to house. Neighbors visited from house to house, and tables were always spread. Ladies took pride in cooking and sharing recipes, because each household had its own style of cooking. There was a taste contest going on between the women. In the church, it was the same way. The women brought baskets of food to church on Sundays. Ladies competed in baking the best cake or making the best potato pie, ice cream, rolls, or decorating the prettiest basket.

Ladies were always in competition. They would sew and make the finest of the finest from cotton sacks. When cotton sacks got old and soft, that meant they had become refined. Beautiful things were made from them.

In those days, ladies were ladies, and gentlemen were gentlemen. The respect flowed, because the ladies knew how to carry themselves in a way to get respect. There was not a lot of cars, but honey, the men opened doors and helped the ladies into the carriages. They asked for the ladies' hands in marriage, and all of the things that a man was supposed to do. This was because of the way the ladies presented themselves.

There is still refined hospitality in the Delta; stop now, look around, think about it. What do you see that you think has changed or needs changing? Maybe you can help with this. Refined hospitality is something that each person needs to enjoy, but your mind must be right. Focus on yourself and others. If we would do this, things would fall into place.

Please don't see me as a person who is asking you to become a slave again. I am just asking you to share some of your good qualities with someone else who might have all of the qualities one can have from his or her own frame of mind, but still can use some of what someone else has to offer. Since we know there are no two people alike, that means surely we can learn from each other. Hospitality is just being friendly. We have always been southern flowers of the south. You must show how friendly you are. Delta's southern hospitality is not only for the folks in or from the Delta; it is for everyone.

We have come a long ways. We have gained a lot, and we have lost a lot. Parents don't seem so be as concerned as they once were. People don't seem to be getting married like they once did. The respect for religion seems different. You cannot allow others to discipline your children like you used to. Of course, that might not have been good anyway, because I recall there were some grown-ups back then I thought were not fair. But now you should be afraid to leave your child with anyone. To go back, it's hard; to go forward, we get misunderstood; we'll just have to take the bitter with the sweet. I would love that Delta hospitality again. We could walk the streets like we walked the roads day and night without someone hurting us. At night if you were out late, someone would walk you home.

My mind goes back to when I was at Alcorn University. Somebody staged a strike at the university, and the dean said to me, "Miss Wells, if you would tell him or her to go back into their dormitories, they would go back." I often wondered why he asked me. Well, anyway, I couldn't tell them to go back because . . . we stayed out there all night, and the next day we were sent home. They gave me a ticket to Robinsonville, and it was about one o'clock in the morning when I got home. It was dark, and I was afraid to get off the bus, but I did. There was a family that lived close to Highway 61 and it took me about one minute to run to their house. I was knocking on that door and one of the sons got up and came to the door. He didn't know where in the world I came from. I told him what happened, and he got up and walked me home with a smile. Now, that was Delta hospitality.

Delta Music

Stomp down! Stomp down! This is the feeling you got and still get when you hear the Delta music. Blues, gospel, and rock and roll—it was that or nothing. Each of the melodies came straight from the heart of man, soulfully with feeling. It was the kind of music that made you move. These artists did not study at any certain college. They were the colleges of music. First, they would hum the tune, sing, and then put it to music on whatever instrument they were using. Blues was on the rise big-time. They found most of the tunes in the Delta Cotton Fields. Late in the evenings or early in the mornings, the hard-core blues came straight from the Delta Cotton Fields. Picking, chopping, and plowing cotton would give you the blues. There were just a few people from the Delta that couldn't sing the blues or play the blues on some kind of instrument.

As you played, people gathered around to listen then they would say, "I believe they have something here." Some of these tunes were found in the midnight hours when young men would go to see the young ladies, and as he walked back home that night, he bellowed out a tune that would make the hair rise on your head. When he got home, he would write the words down and find some kind of instrument to beat it out. Saturday night down at the One Minute where everyone gathered, they would sing and someone would beat it out on a homemade instrument, such as a washboard, string of wire, tin tops, or homemade drums.

The Delta music runs deeply through your veins. It had plenty of soul and feeling. It touches most people who hear it. The melody can really get you going if you listen.

In the Delta, people would chop cotton until 12:00, go to the house, stay for an hour, eat, sing or listen to the radio, and then go back to the fields feeling brand new.

Let us not forget music as a whole. Religious music was strong and is still the base of all music in the Delta. Most of your blues singers came from somebody's church choir. They learned to carry the tune in the church's choir, then came the blues. You would hear people singing religious songs all around the Delta cotton fields. They would even give out a hum and that made you want to shout, I mean shout! Old men, old women, young men, young women, boys and girls could connect or relate to the music, gospel, soul, and blues.

This is one of the things that kept the people of the Mississippi Delta going. You have to feel good about something to keep stress from setting in. Somewhere in the back of people's mind, each tune would get them closer to where they wanted to go, and that was out of the cotton fields.

We didn't think of working on the farm as being a sin; we thought of it as a means to an end. It was a back-breaking kind of work from sun up to sun down. Some of the parents would drag the babies or small children on the back of the cotton sack. Lots of times, the tunes would put the babies to sleep.

Some days you would get tired of working in your field, so you would stop and take a walk. There were fields of people all around, miles and miles chopping or picking cotton, and as you pass each field, you would hear a different tune; sometimes you would stop and listen. In the summer, they would sing one kind of song, and in the fall, they would sing another kind of song. Well, I guess when it's hot, you feel one way, and when it's cold, you feel another way.

I have one brother who should be the best songwriter in the world. All he did was walk. He walked to and from the field all day long, listening and making decisions like, I can't pick or chop cotton for a living. I guess the boy just had the Delta Blues; maybe that was his reason for walking all the time. He went to high school, and four years of college. Received a Bachelor's Degree in Social Studies, went to Vietnam, blessed to come back. He taught school for a while at home, in Tunica. He came to Memphis and started working for the Post Office big-time. He is a Supervisor now.

I enjoyed the tunes so much I decided to sit down and come up with my own Delta stuff. I think I wrote twelve songs and got a copyright on each one. One of these days, the world might get a chance to hear one of my songs. I am like everyone else from the Delta. I make music with whatever I can find, a tin can, washboard, a hair comb with paper over it, clapping of the hands, tapping of the feet—hey just name it, and we did it, and still do.

I used to play the piano to bump my tunes out. First, I was using all the black keys, until I met this lady from the Delta; she is some kind of lady. There isn't anything that she can't do. She still lives in the Delta but teaches here in Memphis. I met her husband, a nice gentleman. I want to thank him for allowing her to come here and work. She has done more for me than silver and gold could do. She taught me how to use black and white keys on the piano. But I was still playing those black keys and singing down. This is another example of the Delta hospitality that I spoke of in a previous chapter. These are my home folks. This is how Delta people are sharing with each other. Don't be surprised when you see me playing piano on TV; this has been one of my dreams. And my friend from Belzona, Mississippi, taught me how to play the piano.

I guess Robinsonville had cried out so long, until the world heard its cry. Now people from all over the world are down there singing the blues and gospel. They are coming by the truckloads. Buses are running day and night; the people can't get there fast enough. Now they are building an airport in Tunica, trying to help get the people there faster. It is a site to see! Vegas, look out. We people of the Delta in Tunica County are out to become equal.

Sometimes now I see children beating on boxes, tables, books, or whatever. I can relate to that, because that is how you get started. You hear it in your mind first. Then you just want to beat that tune out, one way or the other. I had both of my sons taking music, but they really didn't want to do it. I left them alone about it. They told me, "Mom, that's your thing, let us live our own lives." I had to respect that. I forget they were not born and reared in the Delta.

Delta Dancing

In the Delta, when it came to dancing, people always got "low as a toe"; we knew how to cut a rug. We couldn't wait until Saturday night. There were not any sad or poor people, but happy people all night. As far as you could see across the fields, you saw some kind of light calling them into the juke joints. Back then, there was not a lot of shooting and cutting—people were having a good time.

The musical instruments were made from washboards. Guitars were made from two bricks and a string of broom wire, and a bottle was used as they picked. They used two tin tops to beat together. They made flutes by taking a cane and cutting holes on the side and blowing into it to make music. That was what you called a real Saturday band; as time went on, the thing got a little better.

In those days, no one taught you how to dance; you just danced to the tunes. There was no such thing as the wrong step; you just stepped to your own feeling. There were many dances that came in style. To name a few: the Charleston, two-step, slow drag, the Texas two-step, rumble, crosscut saw, fox trot, stroll, and the jitterbug. Ring play dances took care of many of the dances: square dancing, seamore, shoo fly, and many others. But back to the basics, dances you did with one person—were the peck, bad ole hog, cha-cha, boxer noble, applejack, cat, dog, doddie green, twist, chicken, nikki hokie, and the rum boogie. As the time went on, a lot of new dances came around. The line dance, the electric slide, and others came down through many generations. People are still holding on to the release of yesterday. There are things no one can take away from you. Dancing is good exercise for the body. There were not a lot of people dieting back in the day, because they were too busy dancing to gain weight.

The Delta dancing was one that could not be matched. People got on buses and went miles away to enter into dance contests, and they would dance all night until the sun come up.

That was one of the big-time sports back in those days. Both parents never went; one stayed home to take care of the kids. They could smell food cooking miles away before they got to the site.

There were a lot of juke joints around. Some closed about twelve o'clock. The people would leave that one and go to another and another until they got to the hole in the wall and it would stay open all night. They had energy because back in those days; people made corn whiskey, and it kept them jumping all night. When Sunday morning came, they went home, changed clothes, and went to church. Back then, they had a lot of respect for their fellowmen. They could not stay home and sleep; they had to go to church and do their duties.

After working hard in the fields all week, they thought it was all right to go get-j-get-j-yi-yi-yi on a Saturday night. It made it better for them the next week, because they knew they were going to do it again the next weekend.

Dancing has been a part of our Delta traditions for many years. Many people back in the day danced for hobbies. Tap dancing, ring dancing, and line dancing were some of them. They danced both in the church and out. The difference in dancing in the church was that you didn't cross your legs while you danced. You could jump up and down or go side to side but no leg crossing. The rooster strut was a tough dance. My dad said his dad taught it to him. But the toughest dance in my dad's day was getting low as a toe. Papa said, "That was boss!"

I used to dance like my dad, but now I dance like my mom. My mom always did the church dances. My big brother, Mr. Collins Wells, I think can still get low as a toe if he wanted to, but he is still a church man.

The swim was a dance everyone could do—children, grown-ups, and old folks. But what dances could children not do? They really had to teach the grown-ups.

There are a lot of new dances out. I wouldn't start naming them. Each time you turn on TV, you will see someone with a new dance. I don't know if they name them anymore or just move with the feeling, but that's okay. That's the way dancing started. Somebody put some steps together and named them. The ole barnyard dance, the pony paw, and the duck walk all started this way. It's about time that someone starts a dancing school and teaches these dances. Back in the day no one taught people how to dance. When you saw someone doing these steps—ha!—you just started getting up and getting down.

Like today, I see people taking dancing lessons and paying for it. Not like yesteryears, those people had rhythm and their moves were smooth as silk. The songs of today and the music give everybody a different move—like rap—I don't have anything against rap. Everyone is a free spirit when it comes to dancing. You just move like you feel, up, down, around and around, on the floor, upon the wall; whatever comes to the mind of the artist, that is the way it is.

I have young sons; they give me a chance to hear all types of music and see all the latest dances. The older son likes jazz, gospel and country music. The younger one likes rap, gospel, and a little bit of everything. Just last night I heard him say that he wanted to hear a little blues this weekend. He said that he was going to tell his partner to stick in a few blues CDs in the slot; my nephew Archie brought us some by the house so he can pick his choice.

Sometimes I look at Jar and ask myself how did you learn to do the Delta dances, but I guess it is just in his blood. Ty, my older son, dances sometimes.

Back in the day, I went to West Memphis with one of my sisters-in-law and went to this dance hall, and those people danced so hard, they were all just soaking wet. I was looking at them so hard and not taking care of my own business. One of them took my billfold out of my purse. That taught me a lesson. Don't carry your money in your purse when you go out. But I don't think that would have happened at a Delta dance.

Delta Hairstyles

Hairstyles for the woman have always been an important thing. A woman's glory is her hair. As far back as we can go in the beginning, women did not cut their hair. They came up with all kinds of styles. Some wore long styles with their hair hanging down. Some wore their hair pulled up high with curls.

The name of some of the hairstyles were: french roll, pumpy doo, braids, corn rows, rop, shag, ring curls, feather curls, up sweep, humpteem baby, pageboy rap, and fingerwaves.

Men, too, like women took pride in caring for their hair from the beginning of time. Being well groomed was one of the fancies of men. They wore different hairstyles. To name a few: bird in the bush, college cut, fade, shag, gooch, etc.

In those days, your parents or a big sister or brother were the masters. Most of the hair grooming was done at home; they did not have barbershop and beauty shops around then.

Courtship in Those Days

The young men and young ladies usually met at church, because most times, they lived so far and worked so much. They met on the weekends, and they talked at church when they thought they knew each other well enough. He would ask permission from the parents to come and visit the young lady at her home.

If the parents thought he was a nice young man, they gave him permission to visit with her at their home once a week. Then after the family had known the man for a while, and the parents thought he was okay, he'd ask to take the young lady out.

He came on Sunday evening riding in his wagon with his mules pulling to pick up the young lady. She dressed in her fancy dress, hair styled, and high-heeled shoes. He would help her into the wagon, and they would ride along the countryside, and the wind would be blowing, trees would be budding, flowers blooming, and they would enjoy. They would pass other couples as they rode along the countryside. Sometimes they would visit friends there on the plantation, and sometimes they would go to a common meeting place with others and talk. There was a dance held in the town of Robinsonville on Saturday nights. Sometimes the young men would take the young ladies.

Later in the courtship, if marriage took place, there would be a beautiful ceremony. The young men would ask for the young ladies' hand in marriage, and her parents would give consent. As the planning get started, the bride would select her bridesmaid, flower girls, and the others. The groom would select his best man and the others. The planning would go on for about a year. Families would start making dresses, shirts, suits, flowers, the bride's dress and veil. During this time, the bride and groom were so busy that they didn't have time to see each other that much. They were working hard for that big day in the spring. That's when most of the weddings took place.

Finally, that Sunday evening came. Just let me relive it for you. The wedding would be held at the home of the bride, on the porch, about 6:00 PM. People would start arriving in the afternoon about 3:00 until 5:30—bringing cakes, pies, chicken and dressing, punch, ice tea, and hams, and the mother of the bride would make the big wedding cake real tall, most of the time about eight to ten layers. At 5:30, everyone would be gathered. Wagons and buggies would be lined up for miles and miles down the roads. These people would have come from joining plantations around that Delta County. Some came as far as what was referred to as in the hills. Places like Red Banks, Victoria, Byhalia, Marshall County, Tunica's Mhoon Landing, Hollywood, Walls, Lake Comorant, and Memphis, Tennessee, where they had relatives. The bride was hidden away until 6:00 on the dot. She joined her beautiful wedding court. People standing as far around as you could see were quiet and waiting. Everybody was in place at this time. The preacher stepped forward, softly praying, then the ceremony would begin. A broom was placed on the floor before the bride and groom when all saying had been said, then the preacher would say, "Salute the bride"; they would kiss and jump over the broom. Then the cheering and laughter began. Rice was thrown, and people would start shaking hands and kissing the wedding couple. After that, the wedding dinner started for all. The bride and groom would cut the tall wedding cake, and the party would go on until late in the night. When it was over, the people got into their wagons and buggies and went home if they lived near, but those who lived far away waited until the next morning and started on their way home. These kinds of celebrations happened often. Those were happy days for a lot of people.

After all of the wedding celebrations were over, the husband would go and find himself a track of land, then he and his new bride would move onto it and set up housekeeping. The families of the bride and groom would give them enough furniture to furnish the house. They gave chickens, hogs, cattle, and a dog.

Back then, dogs were used to take care of the outside, especially at night. When you heard the dog bark, you knew something was around, so you would get up and look outside. Your father and other men always kept their guns handy. I know my dad was ready to shoot anything. People were afraid to pass our house, but they knew when they moved into their own little house and started a crop and family that they needed to get themselves a dog and gun. What the young lady couldn't cook, she would ask her mom or another lady who lived close to her. The young man was the same way. He could go to his father and find out how to do different things. The groom and bride knew a lot of things themselves because they had worked side by side with their parents. It didn't matter if it were on the farm, or in the house. You learned what skills your parents had and some more. You learned how to make candy from Mrs. Della; you learned how to make jelly, bread, and pickles from Mrs. Jenny. Mrs. Ida taught you how to make good vegetable soup, because she worked near a place called Pots Camp. This is where the big jail was in Mississippi. That is where the real bad people in the Delta went and still go, I believe. She made soup and canned it, so they could feed those inmates.

The young housekeepers had a lot of help back then. The mother and mother-in-law of the young bride made sure that after each baby was born, the new mother did not lose her shape. They taught her how to get a sheet and cut it in half, wrap it around her stomach, and wear that sheet for six weeks; when she came back into the public, she looked the same. She had to eat rice and baked chicken for a month, so she would not develop indigestion. Back then, every lady breast-fed her babies; if the mother ate something that made her sick, it would make the baby sick. The family grew; more and more children came. Finally, they all grew up and went to school, and those parents took on the ways of other parents. The children would grow up and leave.

Delta Marriage

Marriages in the Delta during the late 1800s and early 1900s were amazing. People believed in getting married. They got married at an early age, stayed together, and reared their families.

The families would do what you call giving them a start, which is now called a wedding shower. They gave them pots, pans, and just whatever they needed for the house.

Once they were married, you never heard of a divorce because they were too busy trying to get things straight so that they could make ends meet, and take care of their children and themselves. In those days everybody was about on the same level of living. When they got married, they loved and cared about each other. One could not be jealous at what the other person had; both had about the same thing. They worked together for the good of the whole family. Maybe a few years after they were married, they could buy a few things with the little savings that they had. It took them forever to save up enough money to get a down payment on anything. The first thing they wanted was a nice new bedroom suite, new bedspread, and a new kitchen cabinet. Most people did not have living rooms, dens, or great rooms. Sometimes they had two rooms, maybe three rooms at the most. The husband was busy outside building henhouses, hog pens, and duck ponds, and fences around the yard. The cow needed a pen. The work around the house and in the fields kept the married couple too busy to think of anything else but finishing everything that day and going back the next day.

My thinking now is maybe people have too much free time on their hands. Ladies sometimes need a hobby so when they finished preparing for the husband and children, they would have something to do. They would sew, knit, write, play the piano, plant flowers, and fix their husbands' drawers where they put their socks and other things. They would read over their Sunday school lesson and plant a small vegetable garden. The husband would cut the yard, read over his Sunday school lesson, wash the car, teach his son what he knew about cars, take the family on outings, tell the sons to wear belts on their pants, and go on vacation with the family. The whole family would walk, jog, and watch their diet.

You see, we, Delta women, know how to keep a marriage together. I believe when people get married, they want to be okay. In the Delta, people had fifteen to twenty-five children. My daddy and mom had fifteen children. That was the way the marriage turned out. If the husband or wife left, they never got a divorce. They just went and married someone else. That didn't happen too often. I think only one of my cousins did that. He had seven wives— but that was my cousin; he couldn't see that was wrong, but he could see everything that someone else did.

Delta Cooking

Mississippi Mud

2 (15 oz.) cans black beans, drained
1 teaspoon olive oil
1/2 cup cheese
1/2 tomato
1/2 garlic clove
1 teaspoon chili powder
2 cups cooked ground beef
1/2 cup lime juice
1/2 cup mild picante sauce
1/4 cup chopped onion

Country Glazed Ham

1 cup lemon juice
1 cup brown sugar
1 garlic clove
1 small can cherries
1 ham

Stuffed Green Peppers

1 lb. cooked ground beef
1 garlic clove
1/2 cup milk
2 eggs
1 teaspoon lemon juice
1 tablespoon chopped basil

6 green peppers cut in half
Cover all ingredients with tomato sauce.

Delta Chicken Salad

3 lbs. cooked chicken, black and white or mixed, cut to please
1/2 cup chopped fresh onion
2 chopped boiled eggs
2 cups toasted breadcrumbs
1/2 teaspoon paprika
2 teaspoons ground ginger
1 chopped bell pepper
1 part celery, chopped fine
Miracle Whip

Bar-B-Que Ribs

Soak meat in apple-cider vinegar for 2 hours.

Cook ribs on grill over slow heat until tender.
Sauce: 1 cup brown sugar
1/2 cup honey
1 cup lemon juice
1 chopped onion
1 teaspoon salt
Mix all ingredients together.
Place sauce over ribs.
Place ribs back on the grill and cook for another five minutes.

Delta Southern Fried Chicken

1 whole chicken
Batter: 2 eggs beaten, blended with 1 cup of milk
1 teaspoon salt
1/2 teaspoon garlic powder
Blend well.

Place chicken in the mix.
Let stand for 3 minutes.
Take chicken out and put flour on it.
Place chicken into hot olive oil.
Cook on a low burner.
Turn chicken over as needed until done.

Southern Baked Turkey and Dressing

Wash turkey inside and out.

Place in roasting pan; add 1 onion, 1/2 celery, and 1/2 bell pepper chopped finely. Add 1/2 teaspoon of salt, 1/2 teaspoon of black pepper, 1 teaspoon poultry seasoning, 1/2 teaspoon of garlic powder, pinch of red pepper, pinch of paprika. Cover with aluminum foil, and cook in oven at 350 degrees until done. Take turkey out of roasting pan and set aside. Save turkey stock to add into dressing. Clean roasting pan and set aside for dressing.

Place 2 1/2 cups of self-rising meal, 1 cup self-rising flour, and 1 teaspoon sugar into a mixing bowl, mix well. Add 1 cup buttermilk, 2 eggs, and 1/2 half stick of melted butter, stir well. Pour batter into cast iron skillet with remaining 1/2 stick melted butter. Cook until done.

Crumble cornbread into roasting pan; add turkey stock in a little at a time until you get the right consistency, not soupy. Add in 1/2 container of sage a little at a time; add in extra poultry seasoning, extra chopped onion, celery, bell pepper, and salt. Add in 1 cup of breadcrumbs and 1 can of cream of chicken soup; mix well. Place turkey in center of dressing and stuff some of dressing mixture inside of turkey.

Cook in 350-degree oven until done, occasionally brushing turkey with melted butter so that it can brown beautifully.

Serve with chilled whole or canned cranberries.

Delta Water

The water in the Delta was a thing to remember. Most people used pumps. To help you understand the word pump, I'll explain. They found a place in the earth that was soft enough to drill pipes in the ground. They would drill until they found water. They could hear it running under the ground. Then they would place the pump on the top of the pipe and take the handle up and down until the water came out. If the water didn't come out, you would pour some water in the pump, take the handle up and down to prime the pump, then the water would start coming.

This was some rough water. You could not allow it to set overnight; if so, it turned your bucket an orange yellow. You could not wash the bucket clean with soap and water; you had to use ashes. Ashes were the dust you got from burning wood. The water was used for drinking, bathing, and washing clothes. You could not wash white clothes in this water unless you pumped a barrelful, put ashes in it, and allowed it to set for about two days. Then, it was ready to wash white clothes. If you washed your white clothes before you put in ashes, they would turn yellow, but you could wash the color clothes in it. If you allowed it to set, without ashes, it smelled.

Some families would haul water from the well to drink, cook, and wash with. Some families would set out barrels when it rained and caught water to use for washing clothes. Rainwater could not be used for drinking, because it would make your throat sore. I think you could boil it, and it would be okay.

Delta Insects

Back in the days of the 1800s and up, most people in the Delta feared for their lives. There were so many harmful insects around. Each one carried a different kind of germ. Parents feared for babies and smaller children, because they couldn't tell you if they had been bitten or not. Ticks, fleas, mosquitoes, bed bugs— you name it—were all dangerous.

The Delta parents learned how to make good use of everything. They would make nets to go over the beds at night to keep the mosquitoes from biting them and the children while they slept. Every bed had a mosquito bar over it. It was a thin net that went all over the top of the bed, so you could sleep well at night. Your dad would put screen wire on the windows and the front and back porch to help keep the insects out. When you went outside at night, you wore long sleeves, long dresses or pants to protect yourself from the insects. Back then, mosquitoes didn't carry a lot of germs like they do today. If any insect bites you today, you had better head straight to the doctor to make sure you are okay. We are not as strong and healthy today as the people were back in those days.

Delta Travel

Most traveling in the Delta was done by walking. When the people were not walking, they rode horseback, and with a horse and buggy. They rode on mules, wagons, trucks, and trains, and if they had a little money, they rode the T-Model Ford. But again, most of the time, people traveled by walking.

Truck City

The Delta is just that. Nowadays, everyone in the Delta has some kind of truck, some pick-ups, big trucks—just name them and the Delta has it.

I recall back in the day when it wasn't cool to ride a truck to church on Sunday or when you wore your high-heeled shoes. But now—boy! That's the big thing. You can do a lot of things with a truck. Really, always could. It was just the thinking of the ladies back in the day.

Trucks have taken the place of most of the popular cars. In these times, you are not considered cool if you don't drive a truck.

Delta Gossip

Delta gossip is a term used back in the day, when most people walked where they wanted to go. Some were going to the store, church, neighbor's house, fields—just name it, and they went. Nothing could stop them because they did not have to buy gas. So they walked, stopped, talked, and gossiped. The gossip in those days was good gossip. It wasn't about hurting anybody; it was pretty helpful. Mostly women were into doing this kind of stuff. Men went about their business with their chores. Of course, women had chores, but petty gossip kept them happy and busy. Even though they gossiped, there was a lot of respect around.

There were trains running back then. A lot of times they would go from small towns to small towns, and while they were on the train, they gossiped. That was a little different from turn road gossip, because these people lived far away from each other, but they knew each other. And because they met on the train, they would discuss good gossip. In the older days, that's how a lot of news got around from mouth to mouth. Women did a lot of this, but men did their share of spreading the word.

Gossip was so powerful that they learned to do it far away—they used signs. For example, lowering the flag meant a certain thing; one white shirt hanging on the line meant another thing. A pole with a white piece of material, ringing of bells, one ring, two rings, and three rings all meant something different. A lot of this came down through generations.

Delta gossip nowadays gets around like other places. We have all modern methods and techniques of spreading the word, and it goes fast. E-mail, telephone, broadcasting, radio, fax machines, newspapers, and television are all present today.

We have come a long, long way. The Delta was flat land for miles around, and people took advantage of that. If people today would take advantage of the things around them, they would be better citizens. It's a mountain standing right before you, and you are treating it like a molehill. I know it sounds like it should be the other way around. My point is we don't take enough time with anything. We don't try to see what things are good for. We treat most things as if they were nothing. It's okay to discuss and share your ideas. Maybe some good could come out of everything if we treat it with respect. Whether it is gossiping or just plain discussing. The people in the Delta treated everything as if it were a peach, using the fruit, seeds, and peelings for hogs, and wine, and that meant they really got the good out of it.

If people think it's in the form of gossip, people will listen closer. If someone is speaking, most people can't remember what they said. That's why when I want something remembered, I say it in a low, quiet voice, and everyone hears it.

Delta Men

Angels from Heaven

The gentlemen of the Delta were refined, and still are. They supported their families. They were church-going men. They shared in keeping the schools open. They made sure they had wood, coal, fruit, and milk for the school children. They worked in the church. They were farmers, and they stayed in shape because they did manual labor. They grew tall and strong. They loved their daughters, but their sons were the most important to them, because they kept the family name going. The men of the Delta were instrumental in keeping the families together by making sure everyone knew who was a part of the family, and where the family roots started. They would form a wagon train with about five or six wagons, and the families would load up and travel miles to visit other family members who lived far away.

They provided food for their families by killing hogs and cows, raising chickens, and making sorghum molasses. They grinded corn to make corn for meal. The men of the Delta fished, and they hunted and trapped for minks. Some even made moonshine and homebrew. They plowed the fields, and they planted and chopped cotton. The men of the Delta worked long hours but got satisfaction from providing the best life they could for their families.

Some of the men were not educated, but they wanted their children to get a good education, as they would say. Now I believe as a whole they should have pushed their sons harder, because men are the breadwinners of the family. Sometimes they pushed the girls harder (well, not in my family, because my brothers were precious jewels). The boys in my family wouldn't let me or my sisters drive the car. They were Mr. Untouchables. My dad didn't like them to mistreat us. I still love you, guys, only sometimes it seems to me you have changed too much. You, guys, might need to go back and review the angelic way of the Delta man because your roots don't change. You just need to be reminded. They will probably talk to me about this, but it's not so deep that I can't explain.

All men are jewels; I know that you don't have to be from the Delta. I just happen to have known the Delta men better. This is where I grew up, and what you learned kind of stays with you. My husband was a Delta man, and out of all of the men at the Mason Temple that night, men from all over the world, I go and meet a man from Robinsonville. I still can't believe it; he looked better to me than all of the others. It was probably that Delta hospitality that got me. Believe me, you can only write about what you know.

Men, I want you to know I am one of the best friends you could ever have. I love all men, and I know you are precious. That's why the Lord gave us to you. Keep on treating us with love and care, because we belong to you. If it had not been for you, we would not be here. God made us for you, that is an obligation of ours—to love, respect, honor, and obey you when you are right.

Harvest Time

Harvest time was the crop gathering time. The last days of August was the beginning of harvest. The cotton would open, and two weeks after, everybody got their sacks together to start picking. Then singing, humming, and whistling started. This made picking cotton an easy task. This crop was planted in March or April. The cotton came up in May or June. The chopping started in June, and it went on until the last of August. Children went to school the last of August, all of September, and October. The last of October, all of November, and part of December, or maybe all. Then school started again in January and ended in May.

We went to school seven months a year. Later, we started going nine months. That was Delta style. Students went to high school the same way. The first high school that was built in Tunica County for the blacks was in 1952. There were two private high schools in Tunica and one in Pritchard. If you didn't have money, you could not attend. Some did, and some didn't. There were people who finished high school and college, but they had to leave Tunica County.

For many years, Tunica County was the poorest county in the United States of America. With thirty-seven millionaires, only one was black.

The people raised their own food, made their own clothes, or bought them.

There were certain wash days, and everybody washed on that day. As far as you could see, white sheets and other clothes would be flying high. The smell of the sheets at night after a fresh wash and a day in the sun was enough to relax you and put you straight to sleep.

Harvest time was not just for cotton, but for peaches, pears, peanuts, and sweet potatoes. We found a way to get all of these done. You picked the pears in the fall. When night came, you sat and peeled pears half of the night. When you finished peeling the pears, you cut the core out of the pear and then you sliced them. You would then put them into a big pan and pour five pounds of sugar on them that was for a bushel. You let them set for a day and a night in the sugar and allowed them to make their own juices. Then you set the pears on the stove and allowed them to cook until they were brown and syrupy. That is what we called pear preserves. We ate that with breakfast in the morning. I remember breakfast like it was yesterday. I remember having hot biscuits, ham, scrambled eggs, preserves, milk, and sometimes orange juice. Mom never had to wake us up. The smell of breakfast did it for her. The peaches and other foods were done the same way. That was a farm girl and boy's job during harvest time.

I recall one day we were picking cotton and my high-school principal came up to our house, and we were in the fields. I had on my jeans, a long-sleeved shirt, sun hat, and gloves. He looked at me and said, "Mildred, you don't look like a city girl today, you look like a farm girl." He always said funny things, I thought, but one of my classmates didn't want me to laugh at his jokes. Every time he told a joke, I would be ready to laugh, and she would be watching me to see if I were going to laugh, and when I did, she would tell me that I was the one who kept him telling those not-so-funny jokes. She was a mess. She even said she could not get her lesson unless she was sitting next to my brother. She wasn't a farm girl. She lived in the old subdivision in Tunica.

Harvest time was the laid-by time. I guess it meant that work was over for a while.

BRIDGING THE GAP BETWEEN THE HOME, SCHOOL AND COMMUNITY WITH EMPHASIS ON "PUTTING PARENTS BACK TO BEING PARENTS"

AND

LOWERING THE STRESS LEVEL IN THE HOME

Author
Mildred Wells Dunn

CONTENTS

DEDICATION

This book is dedicated with love to my two sons, TyJuan Wells Dunn and Jarvis DeVor Dunn, my nephew, Steven Wells, who motivated me to write "Bridging The Gap Between the Home, School and Community," my family and friends.

Foreword

You may add to any page or paragraph words, phrases, or sentences that will help you best understand what has been written. Although we might not ever meet, help me with my dream. Help me in "Bridging the Gap Between the Home, School, Church, and Community with Emphasis on Putting Parents Back to Being Parents." A young lawyer on Beale Street once looked at me and said, "You are sincere about what you are saying and doing. I will not charge you anything." Boy, was I glad! I had him to look at the script because I had just about gone broke on "Bridging the Gap Between the Home, School, Church, and Community." There have been others who said to me, "What are you trying to do?" And my reply would be, "I know—it's just hard for me to make you understand." Readers, I hope you will understand what I am trying to say and do. Let me make it plain. I am trying to help somebody, hoping I will also receive equally what my readers receive. I am thankful for my family tree, but aren't we all? I would love for every American family and family of this world to add "Bridging the Gap Between the Home, School, Church, and Community" to their library. I would love to hear from some of the readers to see what they think about it. It has taken a while to complete this work. I feel like there will be more books on this same work.

Each of us in our own way can bridge the gap. We do not have to look for any help. Just think of things we can do to help someone.

Acknowledgements

Tri-State Defender and the Commercial Appeal

I would like to take this opportunity to thank all of the people who helped me. I especially thank Mr. Keith Williams, Jarvis DeVor Dunn, TyJuan Wells-Dunn, Mrs. Brenda Alston, Mrs. Cynthia A. Gentry, and Ms. Eunice McNeal.

Introduction 1

As I sit and listen to parents, teachers, ministers, children, and other community people, everybody seems frustrated because they think there is not a solution to the problems.

"I can't do anything with my children."

"We are loosing out."

"How far will this go?"

"Everybody is under pressure."

We must come together as one body, the home, school, and community, to eradicate stress. Each of us in our own way can help. Therefore, we must come together and bridge the gap.

Stress is the number-one enemy. It causes students to drop out of school, teachers to become short of patience, and parents to become abusive. It affects all of us in some way. It might not happen in your home, but it's worldwide, so we all feel the pressure. Think of the pressure in the world today. We can't get rid of it. But we can learn how to deal with it more effectively.

My reason for starting this program is to let people know they can become stress-free. I was a victim of stress for two years. It took physical fitness, neighborhood work, Sunday school, walking three to four miles a day, riding bikes, and aerobics to relieve me of that pressure. I know a lot of people will agree with me that this works.

I hope that "Bridging the Gap Between the Home, School, Church, and Community" will help us come close to eradicating stress in the home. Doing this on a small scale will help. We will see improvement and will be able to improve throughout the world. It's needless to continue in the same direction when you see destruction is at hand.

Introduction 2

It has been too long since I attempted to bridge the gaps. Minutes and seconds are too long to be absent from such a task.

"Bridging the Gap Between the Home, School, Church, and Community" must become a way of life if we plan to succeed. We, the now generation, are in control and should learn how to communicate effectively with each other. We don't have a lot time to look back at the past or look to the future. Of course the past gives us a foundation to build on or delete. "Bridging the Gap Between the Home, School, Church, and Community" takes in everybody.

We, the people of these United States and the world, deserve the right of "Bridging the Gap Between the Home, School, and Community with Emphasis on Putting Parents Back to Being Parents." With this in mind, we will be able once again to dedicate—we will be able to concentrate—we will be able to hallow these grounds. Even though the people before us were not plagued with the problems our society faces today, every generation has its problems. The world has long stood and our problems have become intense!

Bridging the gap is the missing link that tells what happens to our society. Homes, schools, and churches took a big dive in the wrong direction and have continued in this way for much too long. Bridging the gap is a good way to get our families back together again. All of us can testify to the fact that something has gone wrong, and now we know what it is. Our communities, which consist of the homes, schools, and churches, can help to set things in order.

This "now generation" must admit that the home must take another look at the family. Home is where everything has its beginning. You must have training to do most jobs. However, our parents did it by trial and error hoping that they would succeed.

This leaves our darling children, the most important beings on earth, to suffer.

There should be multi-training programs for our parents. It should be placed in the school curriculums as well as English, math, etc. Bridging the gap is a method that will involve all people especially dealing with the homes, schools, churches, grocery stores, shopping malls, doctors' offices, beauty and barber shops, street corners, store fronts, laundry mats, etc. "Bridging the Gap Between the Home, School, Church, and Community" will make us aware of our need to improve our lifestyles.

Before becoming a parent, we need to develop an organized mind. Check to see if we can function under certain pressures. Putting parents back to being parents simply means taking on your responsibilities and the things parents should do for children. Know where they are at all times. Make sure they stay in school. Make sure they read more. Be the best parent you know how to be before your children. Parents have the children first. Therefore, they will have to lay the cornerstone. Please teach them to obey. That is the first step in following simple directions.

Our schools get our children after they leave home. I want the school to know it's okay to question the home about a four—or five-year-old child or younger, because the home is supposed to help prepare the child for school. We, as parents, do most things our children want us to do. If you don't know what your child should know before he or she starts school, check with other parents, your local schools and day care centers. May I inform you of the most important thing—make sure he or she is told to finish one task before going to another task. This is one of the ways we can make sure they are listening.

The churches have a very important role to play. Get involved with the whole person or family not just on Sunday. Open the doors daily for people who need counseling, clothing, food, day care for young children, or whatever. The church does not need to charge for everything. It is fine to build these fine big buildings, but how well is the public being benefited?

I have shared "Bridging the Gap Between the Home, School,

Church, and Community" with many people. It is being used in a lot of cities and states. I shall not be satisfied until it's used throughout the world. It gives me joy to know that I have helped the world to be a better place.

Philosophy

Stress is a pressure, force, or strain which is interrelated with all body parts. It is a process of deteriorating the body and mind. People undergoing stress should consult a doctor or other trained professionals. Strategies should be adapted to the emotional and social development of an individual. Stress instruction should enable each individual to relax and function effectively.

Resources

The churches, schools, boards of education, police department, city hall, mayor, fire department, other educational agencies, television, radio, and the community as a whole can help bridge the gap.

The churches will be used for centers. I'll be asking all churches to open their doors two to four hours a week for tutoring services for our students. We plan to have four to five tutors for each center from one to six grades placing emphasis on Reading Comprehension and whatever is needed. Tutors will be provided from seven to twelve grade in English and Math.

All churches in the city or cities will be asked to supply us with the necessary facilities to aid our students. The principals and teachers will be asked to give out information concerning student progress to parents and students and inform them where the centers will be located. The mayor and city hall will be asked to correlate "Bridging the Gap Between the Home, School, Church, and Community" into their plans so we can service the city better. Other educational agencies will be asked to look in on the program and give us a boost by giving a write-up. Television and radio will be asked to help get this information out to the public. The community as a whole will help look out for the youngsters during the summer months—give them jobs or help create jobs.

Self-discipline—one is expected to have on hand information about self-control after participating in this program. Evaluation—we will check with the police department, hospitals, and fire department, schools, and others to see if there is a decline in certain areas where stress caused problems. Check with hospitals and fire department about children being left alone, bed fires from drinking, child abuse, etc. We will have pastors of all churches to pass out forms and let all the people help evaluate the program. The pastors of the centers will service a consultant to help with the program.

> "Stress is to the body and mind as
> acid is to the garment."
> —Mildred Wells-Dunn

This program has been designed to teach you how to reduce and deal with stress.

"Bridging the Gap Between the Home, School, Church, and Community" will become one organization worldwide. The mission of this organization is to enhance the relationship of the church, community, and school.

The gap that has recently surfaced between these institutions must be bridged if our society is to thrive and survive. The group was organized in 1990 and has operated with the assistance of community volunteers. These volunteers have served as tutors, motivational speakers, counselors and mentors for the at-risk students in our community. The volunteers consist of several professional educators, doctors, ministers, and parents of our community. These same people make up the governance body of the organization: "Bridging the Gap Between the Home, School, Church, and Community."

Our specific community is within the Mallory Heights—Fowler Homes Boys Club area. We have approximately seventy-five thousand citizens, twenty-five schools, and twenty-five churches. Our community has in recent years experienced a tremendous growth in violent criminal activity. There is compelling evidence of a breakdown between the family and school and the school and community. We see the role of the church as one of diminishing in quality as well. Therefore, we have appealed to the religious organizations in our area to assist us in bridging our community back together and thereby eliminating the rising tide of crime. We have received the support and cooperation of the schools and civic organizations as well. Everyone acknowledges that if we work together, the quality of life will improve for all citizens in the area and in all of Memphis and the world.

Goals and Objectives of Project

1. To improve the high-school graduation rate in Memphis
2. To reduce the high-school dropout rate in Memphis
3. To establish better relations between the home, church, and school
4. To motivate school age children to be successful in life
5. To reduce the criminal activity in Memphis and particularly the Fowler Home—Lauderdale Subdivision, thereby increasing the quality of life for all Memphians
6. To raise the consciousness of at-risk students to their parents, teachers, etc.
7. To provide basic employment skills, tactics, and opportunity

These goals should be accomplished in a variety of ways:

1. Motivational activities, speakers, exposure, small group discussions, mentoring and shadowing
2. Institutions in the community will serve in the following capacity: Schools will recommend and refer at-risk students; churches will provide facilities and support staff

Community residents will provide their service and time at least two-third of reduction in cost. The economic impact of this project is both immediate and rewarding. Business establishments will be less likely to experience break-ins, vandalism, etc. Employment skills should yield employed citizens. Motivation should foster positive attitudes, thereby changing and improving the employment skills of our citizens. Some encouragement to become enterprisers will be encouraged.

MILDRED WELLS-DUNN, the author of this innovative idea, will be the project manager. Her qualifications are extensive. She is a minister, school teacher, parent, a graduate of Alcorn University, and a public school educator for more than thirty-two years. Most of which were spent in the Whitehaven area. She is widowed, a minister and pastor of the Mt. Ever's Cathedral Church of God in Christ, and the mother of two teenage sons.

The success of our efforts will be determined primarily by the statistical facts. We will keep and provide careful records, tracking each participant, school records, criminal statistics, and employment data, and the base line data will be used for comparative analysis. If these statistics are impacted positively and if our community institutions come together and bridge the gap, we can save our children, therefore, saving the future of Memphis and the world.

Goal

To increase and foster a working relationship between the home, school, and community

OBJECTIVES

1. To identify barriers between the home, school, and community
2. To be of assistance to single parent families (Male/Female Image)
3. To increase the academic achievement of at-risk students
4. To increase the social, economic, and cultural levels of program participants

Parents Are Our Best Resources

1. Single mothers who lived in the housing projects can be trained to be truant officers.
2. Single mothers who live in the housing projects can implement an after-school program within the complex to assist children with homework without distractions and with supervision.
3. Single mothers can start an aerobic class to relieve stress as well as tone the body.
4. Children around the world should have a right to read for enjoyment along with their parents.
5. Parents should check on children at different times during the night, making sure they are safe.
6. Leaving home upset can lead parents and children to be upset and stressful throughout the day.
7. We, the adults of the world, are more than able to provide our children with a good and healthy life.
8. The family that prays together stays together. I want to see prayer back in the schools, but if not the schools, surely the home.
9. We can't give up because there is still hope!

Other Ways To Raise Donations
(Other Than Grants)

1. Collection boxes in each church—Encourage members to give donations on Sundays.
2. Banquet—Using ads, patrons, and auctions.
3. One-time enrollment fee for students able to pay—$5.00.
4. Bake sale—Involving the communities.
5. All centers come together quarterly with a fund-raising project.
6. Car wash—Involving the communities.
7. Aerobic classes—$2.00 enrollment fee.

BRIDGING THE GAP
BETWEEN THE HOME, SCHOOL AND COMMUNITY REFERRALS

AFTER SCHOOL ACADEMY

Time _____ Weekdays _____

Saturdays _____

TUTORIAL
ENRICHMENT
HOMEWORK

Name _____

Telephone Number _____

School _____

Area of Need _ _____

CENTERS LOCATED AT
AREA CHURCHES AND FACILITIES

1.

2.

3.

4.

5.

6.

7.

8.

BRIDGING THE GAP BETWEEN
THE HOME, SCHOOL AND COMMUNITY

MILDRED WELLS–DUNN

Dear Parents,

We feel that everyone in the city and Shelby County should have a high-school education by the year 2009. If you are interested in taking the G.E.D. Test, please return this letter signed to your Resident Manager.

Respectfully,
Mildred Wells–Dunn

_____

Resident's Signature

_____

Resident's Telephone Number

Parents Are Our Best Resources

So many times when we are seeking information about a child we need to start with the parents. They can go farther into a child's background than anyone. The more you know about the family's history, the better you can understand a child. Some things children do are understood when the person in charge understands the family's background.

Parents are able to go back many years before the child was born. I am not saying children are hard to understand. Children inherit things from parents. This is why it is so important for people to know about the family tree and background. Parents must understand the world is depending on them to start the ball rolling again by being the best parents they know how to be. Parents, start working with your children when he or she first starts paying attention to people and objects.

We should never leave parents out when it comes to their children. They know their children better than anyone else does. Let the world give proper respect to parents.

Single Parents

Single parents are just as effective as two parents. It's true children can profit from both parents, but when there is just one parent, children will have just as much respect. Respect for a parent comes from the role the parent plays. Many times, this makes a child strong or more independent because he or she knows Mother or Daddy needs his or her assistance. This does not apply to all but surely some.

Single parents are good role models for children because it's the love and respect the parent gives to a child that is important. When you see children being disobedient, it's because they are suffering from the lack of parental love. We, as parents, can modify our love and care for our children by listening to their problems and trying to find the best solution together. Parents never should talk to children when they are angry. I know it seems hard not to correct a problem on the spot, but if you are angry when you are talking to your child, you will not give them the best advice.

Parents Should Check On Children For Safety

Checking on children should be a major priority whether babies or teens. Babies are quick to run a temperature. This should be dealt with as quickly as possible. Know your babysitter. Keep close check on small children playing outside.

Teens need to be cared for almost in the same way. We know there are so many things they can do for themselves, but they still need your attention at home and school.

Leaving Home Upset
Can Cause A Stressful Day

Make sure before you or any family member leaves home, he or she is calm. Just one "stressed out" person in a workplace, or in school, or wherever, stressed out can cause the whole day to go wrong for a lot of people. This is unfair for whoever is around you. This is what happens when people are not feeling well. It's hard for them to take the next person's feelings sincerely. If you are sick, it's best to rest and see a doctor. But if it is being upset, try to get it straight before you leave home. Your peers will thank you, and you will be glad you did.

Parents or others should not leave home upset. It causes the workplace, church, school, etc. to go wrong. Some form of physical exercise can help one to become calm before he or she leaves home.

How Long?

How long will we as parents sit back and see our children carried off to jail? When are we as parents to come to grips with ourselves? We must know that we are to blame for our young children. Know where your children are. Know where your knives and guns are. Keep them under locks and keys. Check your children before they leave home for school. All of these things come under the heading of being a parent or being in charge.

The role that parents play in the home gives signals to children as to whether or not they can disobey. None of us are perfect, but sometimes we need to change our methods. It is very important that the family sits down together once a week and make plans. Allow the children to have input into the decision-making. Let them help you find out why certain things don't work well. They will know that their ideas and feelings are important from being involved.

Our children are our present, past, and future. We need to provide them with hope, faith, and charity. We are strong; we can do all of these. Parents inspire children and they want to be like mother and father. We will never achieve our goals for a better world unless the parents become 100% involved with the family.

Parents must rededicate their lives and once again become in control of the home. It is our obligation to give our children the best we have, and they will return it back to us. We can not expect anymore than we give. Our children are tired of trying to be parents. They have to put themselves to bed, get themselves up, cook the food, and see after each other that is our job.

Putting Parents Back
To Being Parents

Too long we, as parents, have sit and let everybody take control of our children. This is the reason we are losing them. It is essential for the good of the children that parents stay involved and close to their children. No one can take the place of a parent.

Other people are just assistants. Teach them love and respect for their fellowmen, but always return home because this is where the real love is. If we don't take this in consideration, we stand the chance of losing our children to the world for material things and not real love.

So many times you hear parents say, "I am lost." "My child will not obey." "John is the cause of him doing wrong." "Somebody needs to stop all bad people in the streets." "These schools are just places to ruin children." "Peer pressure." Let's get real parents and admit these are avenues for us. We just hate to sit down and get firm with our children. I have had parents say, "Well, I don't want to make them hate me." Later when the child's life is messed up, he or she will hate you anyway. If you took control before something happens, the hate will turn to love later in life, because the child will realize you did care. If you don't try to correct the child and let him or her go on, later in life it will be hate and hurt. These together will be more difficult.

As parents, we can not and will not ever be "problem free." We just have to find ways to deal with them. There are 101 ways to deal with one problem, and if they don't work, press your way. One thing we as parents have in our favor is time. When the child is born until fifteen or sixteen, do everything you can to keep him or her straight with the love and respect that go with rearing children. By the time they reach seventeen or eighteen, these things will be a part of them and they can do whatever they want to do whenever the need arises. We have come too far to give up on our children. The only thing we need to do is give them that tender love, care, and understanding. I know everything is moving fast.

In some cases it takes both parents working two jobs leaving the children alone to do the best they can. When you are rearing children, try to work one job. Get what you need not what you want until later when the children are old enough to do something for themselves. A sad cry and a bleeding heart in the night is not fair to anyone. It can not be stressed enough: parents are the most important people in a child's life. Don't see me ruling out homes or large houses, food, clothing, jobs, or material things. These things will always be there for us. But our children grow up, and soon they will be gone, and we can't turn back the hands of time. So, let us do what we can for them while they are growing up.

"Parents United" simply means that we are going to join hands throughout the world, door to door, street to street, community to community, city to city, state to state, and be supportive of each other. If it is to be done, we will have to do it! We sat back too long waiting on someone to do it for us. Well, who else is responsible for your child or children? Parents, we can bridge the gap. We do whatever we want when the time comes. When we join forces, there will not be any place to put the blame, all will feel responsible. Remember, we are the same generation that has gone to the moon, conquered the oceans and weathered the storms.

"Parents United" means getting back to the basics and (now beyond) because we have somewhat gotten away from a few family traits. The whole family used to be involved in school, church, chores, breakfast, dinner, family outings, etc. Now, each one goes his or her way. We must come back together in the home first, then the community will be at peace again. We, the community must set up healthy things for the young people—boys' and girls' club, scouts, etc.

Most of our children are unafraid because they are unaware. They don't know what causes what. Most of the time they don't mean harm, but it turns out to be harm because they carry small things too far. With all of us working together, we can win. We built this society. We need to stop thinking of our society as one we just live in. We all created this for our children. It is time that we think of a plan to improve it and put that plan into action.

When it comes to marketable skills, we as parents have those because no one has to teach you to be a parent. We could use more but that comes with the birth of a child. The age does not matter. Once a child is born, you become a mother or a father. I feel that we should stop telling our young people that babies are having babies. We should tell them that at any age you bear a child, you become a responsible parent and you must take on that responsibility. That will give them a chance to make a decision about whether or not they want to be a responsible parent at the age of fourteen or fifteen and take on all of these responsibilities, or whether we should wait and prepare ourselves for a job and get married and then become parents. The decision is going to be up to them; but let us, as parents, try to help them make the right decision. When it's their time, they can help their children make the right choice. As long as parents say to children "babies are having babies," they are going to become parents at an early, irresponsible age, with grandparents sharing all of the responsibilities. When we let them know they will not be referred to as a young girl but mother, or not a young boy but father, and they don't go out and play around, they come home and become a parent. I think our children will think more about what they are doing and will be able to make better choices. They will wait until they are responsible before they rear a family.

Parents, know where your children are at all times. Do not let them leave unless you know where they are going. Make sure you check on them by making a call or showing up at the place. This shows you are concerned, and you are protecting your child because he or she knows you are going to check. Then he or she will come closer to doing right. Try to know who your child's or children's friends are for many reasons. Parents should be concerned about their children. We know when the homes are out of control, the whole neighborhood is in trouble and it spreads. If we can just join forces and keep our homes together, we will have less stress in the schools, workplaces, etc. A family is a two-way project. This is where each one shares everything.

The whole family consists of mother, father, grandparents, greats, aunts, uncles, cousins, nephews, and nieces. It is so important for children to understand about the whole family. This is where the reunions come in, birthday parties, weddings, and other family gatherings so kin can get to know each other. All of us know that is important. Never get too busy for your family. Listen to what is being said at all times. I don't care how a subject sounds, if it is brought up, it is important to that person.

"Parents United" can help our children reach their potentials with the proper guidance. Sometimes they have short attention spans, but this should be expected. "Bridging the Gap Between the Home, School, Church, and Community with Emphasis on Putting Parents Back to Being Parents" is a general concept for the world. United is the only way we, as people, (not as races but people), are going to be able to get homes back together again. A fact is a fact, and it can not be erased. Somewhere we changed. But that is in the past. We are ready to do whatever is necessary to set our homes in order. It must start with the parents. So, parents, get together, have meetings, plan on which ways we are going. Let our home, school, and community go in the right direction. The Christian Arenas (churches) should be able to play a big part in this. It's okay for the pastors to come out before Amazing Grace on Sundays! I remember my grandfather, Bishop E. Cottrell, the bishop of the CME Church, did a lot of this in his lifetime. I recall reading about when he and other bishops went to England in the 1800s, meeting with people to share ideas. We must continue some of the good things our forefathers did. They paved the way for us, not for us to just sit and enjoy, but for us to take up where they left off.

"Parents United" is created for individual homes. You can sit within the area of your own home and come up with the answer to family problems. If we are looking for the missing link, it's discipline, and that starts in the mother's womb. So, mothers, while you are carrying these children, think of positive, good thoughts. Be as pleasant as you can be. Try and keep the right frame of mind. Eat the right foods, fruits, milk, vegetables, vitamins, or whatever it takes to make a healthy child. The father plays the same important part. Keep a healthy body and mind, fathers. You too are responsible for the health and welfare of these babies. What you put into your bodies before these babies are conceived plays an important part. Babies inherit traits from their mother and father. Any parent who neglects his or her duty as a parent—man, woman, or animal—should remember there were good parents before him or her.

Some people feel that the more degrees you have, the better parent you will make. Degrees have nothing to do with being a parent. I'm not saying don't get degrees; by all means do so. But you are who you are before anything is added. I want all people to understand no one in this world is any more "on the ball" than anyone else. It's how you apply yourself. They are not any better parents than you are, and all you have to do is be the best parent you can be. Make no mistake, the child has to come first. By that I mean being born or adopted; this is when the real feeling comes for a parent.

Let us stop programming our young people by talking about them not being the good parents. It's our fault. Let us set good and positive examples for our young people. They are what we have made them. They see us come and go, and sometimes the roads we have taken are not straight. However, we have time to straighten them out by parents becoming united, and when I say parents, that's leaving no parent out. I am speaking of grandparents, uncles, aunts, cousins. The idea is for all of us to become united in this world and set sisterhood-brotherhood ringing.

We can be "Bridging the Gap Between Home, School, and Community" when we as parents unite and put the home first. Again, home is the place where everything starts. So as the morning comes, we start going our separate ways: to schools, to workplaces, and other places in the community. If you are fine when you leave home—child or parent—when you meet with your peers, everything will be fine. But if you leave home upset, your day cannot go right.

Some of the things that make the home all right are (1) freedom from stress—how to do that is by knowing your family members (know that when something is wrong with one of us, something is wrong with all of us); (2) go places together, do things together; (3) don't always have all of the answers—sit as a family and work out the answers together, let everyone feel a part of the planning; (4) always let some member of the family know where you are going or who is coming to visit you. With these kinds of things going on in each home across the nation, we can't help but bridge the gap between home, school, and community. All parents will have started back to being parents.

We must admit that when we don't do our duty, it puts pressure on the whole world. There's no such thing as "I will move away and be in peace." What affects one of us affects all of us. The time is now. Let us stop where we are, turn around, and go back. We must start here this day and change our methods. We should be better prepared now, because we have almost seen the end result but not completely. I feel like this is enough for us as parents to unite, join hands, and carry on in a society that just had a new birth. If we can just believe this, then our coming days will be much brighter. Our children will be much safer, our parents will be less stressful, the world will be much sweeter, our street corners will be safe again, our jails will turn into higher learning institutions, and our churches will not be places where people simply gather. Our schools will be about the business of educating our children. It will be an enchanted world because our values will be in the right places.

"Parents United" will set the behavioral pattern for our society. Since the beginning of time, we have not been inferior and are not now. In our changing society, we might be a little slow to catch up, but all in all, we have done okay, but we are going to do better. As we speak to people, they too will observe it's time to unite from door to door, house to house, street to street, neighborhood to neighborhood, city to city, and throughout the world.

I believe any knowledge we have to share with each other should be shared. It's okay if they take it, use it, and don't give you credit. Both of you will profit, you and the user, because getting the word out is so important. Let me reassure you that all of us have talents or a talent, and there's nothing wrong with using it. That should be and is the reason why we, as parents, should join hands all over the world to help each other. I would hate to think that no one "pitied my groan," meaning, for one reason or the other no one wanted to share my ideas.

When Night Comes . . .

When night comes, every child within a household should be accounted for before a certain hour. No parent should go to sleep with children out, unless they know they are in safe hands, and sometimes this does not work. Nothing less than knowing exactly where your child or children are should be accepted. No parent should be made to feel guilty. You are not in this alone; we are together. Whatever happened in the past, put that behind you now, and know that you have friends in whatever your struggle is. You will not need a lawyer to plead your case or a doctor to come to your bedside as often now that we are united. Stress will be eliminated.

School

Our schools are precious for our darling children, and we, as parents, take our hats off to principals, teachers, board members, schools superintendents, etc. for the fine jobs they are doing with our children. We, as parents, working along with the school, should make everything okay again. People can no longer say students are graduating from high school and can't fill out an application. We, as parents and teachers, are going to see that this doesn't happen. I know our children can succeed with the proper help.

I want the world to think with me for a minute. It appears to me that we stop our children before we get them started. Kindergarten through third grade could be greatly enhanced. Number one, take away the A, B, C, D, and F grades. Stop failing students and make students feel good about themselves. This is what can be done. Go "non-grade" for kindergarten through third grades. Have goals and objectives that a child should learn before he or she can complete a level. When those goals and objectives are met, move to the next level. This will take away failing students. No one likes to be a failure, and this will not take away the child's pride. Use a checklist to mark off progress. Children will be reading, spelling, using phonics, or whatever it takes to reach the level equivalent to third grade.

Start in the fourth with letter grades. By then, the students will have built up self-confidence and never experience failure. By the time they finish sixth grade, they should have been taught all basic concepts and subjects. Seventh through twelfth grades should be a review. Children learn faster at an early age; therefore, all things should have been introduced to them. This will make high school easier and you will have fewer dropouts and less stress. Seventh, eighth, ninth, tenth, and eleventh grades are too late to introduce any concept. Some will learn it, and others won't. This is what makes it hard for students. By this time in a child's life, so many other things have come into place. They have many things to deal with: sometimes family problems or teenager problems, and a new concept just doesn't go over well.

We, as adults, need to show more respect to our children at all ages. I have heard too many adults talk or put young people down. I know adults don't know everything, but most of us know how to respect the next person. We are supposed to be role models for our children. A lot of times, children and students are just giving back to us what we have given to them. If we, as teachers, teach nothing, they give us nothing back. If we as teachers and parents use love and respect while expecting discipline and rewarding our children for good behavior, we will receive the same thing back. Sometimes it's hard for us to understand where we went wrong. Remember children who obey parents at home usually follow simple directions and follow simple discipline rules at school. That is the reason why the home and school must work together for the good of all of us.

SCHOOLS

Schools should be everywhere—street cars, shopping malls, churches, grocery stores, beauty shops, laundromats, parks, and playgrounds. One might say, "How can this happen?" But this is what has to happen if we expect to come up in education. **Churches** have classes set up in the afternoon and on Saturdays for two or three hours. People will be glad to have some place to leave their children that is safe.

Grocery stores—while parents are shopping, have an area set up for two or three hours of instructional time. This will keep students from running around the store getting hurt.

Parks—have a section where young high-school men and women can give instructions as well as have fun. Children love outside fun and games incorporated into education.

Playgrounds—at each game on the playground, require children to learn a different skill before he or she can participate; let it be easy and fun but still learning.

Street buses or L trains—have packages in the back of each seat containing questions and answers; let it take about ten minutes.

Shopping malls—all areas can be used. In stores, have an area set up with learning materials in each store. Parents can leave children there while they shop. Along the long corridor, have learning areas set up. Make all of the learning somewhat fun. Parents will be able to go and shop for clothing, and someone will be in charge of the children.

Beauty and barber shops—have an area for children when you are working on the clients. Let them do formal learning, and the kids won't be in your chair turning around or taking them apart.

Laundromats—set up an area where they can work in or with games. These things must be done in a quiet matter while parents clean clothes.

Please make sure all people used in these areas are very responsible people. In fact, sign children in and sign them out. Don't just leave them any place. In learning places, make sure you have responsible people working in these areas.

The big question is, "Where will you get the money from?" Check with your mayor of the city, state representative, and congressman. I believe you can set up corner learning centers for people who like to gather and talk, mostly grown-ups, and fix a center for them. Find money within your city or state because all of us are trying to pull education back to its highest level. Education is the best friend we have. Without it, the world can not move forward. Sometimes we wonder what is wrong, and we are falling behind. People can't get the job they want or need. The more educated we become, the more jobs we can establish for our world. If someone comes up with a bright idea, don't put it on the back burner because it's not yours.

The Homeless

The homeless should not exist. There are enough vacant apartments, houses, and school buildings for everyone to have a place to live. This is a blessed world in which we live. Those of us who can, should help those who can't. These buildings can be fixed so each family can have an apartment with three bedrooms, two bathrooms, kitchen, great room, den or living room, and closets. Each large unit should have two people in charge to make sure everything goes okay. We are our brothers' and sisters' keepers. It seems hard sometimes, but we know life is not easy. I find it hard to accept the fact that people should be homeless and hungry. As we bridge the gap between the home, school, and community, we will leave nothing unturned. We have the resources. This land in which we live is rich.

The Christian Arena needs to get more involved. I remember when the churches were used for most things. It was open seven days a week and at nights. I went to school at Christian Spring Missionary Baptist Church at Bowdre, Mississippi, one mile below Robinsonville, Mississippi, now Sam's Town, from first grade until I was eighth grade. There was only one room, and at night, they had box suppers (now we call them banquets). On Sunday, church was held there. We lived three miles away and walked every day to school. This is in Tunica County near Memphis, Tennessee. Back then, we did not have phonetic programs, planned curriculums, teacher's manuals for the textbooks. Most of the books did not have backs on them. Everybody taught you how to read. Mom, papa, sisters, Sunday school teachers, pastor, whoever. Everybody felt responsible for everyone else.

Those days will return and with all of us working together they will return! This time, we will have a solid foundation, because education will be added to our Christian Arenas and they will be equipped with educational departments, gymnasiums, educated people, professors, degree teachers, mothers, fathers, and pastors, and let us not forget love. We, as a people, can make a difference, but we must humble ourselves. With these things working together, no one will be hungry or homeless. The war is on and the fight is ours. We can not decide any longer who should do what. Each of us should make sure we do our part. All of us have talents. Sometimes we have to keep trying things until we find what we do best. Once you find out what you do best, work with it.

When each of us goes back to the first law of nature, which is self-preservation, we find that we have to take care of ourselves first, then we will be able to help others. Let us get busy in our homes, neighborhoods, and all over our cities "Bridging the Gap Between the Home, School, Church, and Community" It is the job of all us to do this. No matter where you work, live, or you attend school, this struggle is for the whole world. "Bridging the Gap Between the Home, School, Church, and Community" is a renaissance. This is the birth of a new world. When all of us can join hands again and don't have to worry about a lot of things we are going to correct. Our children will be able to play safely outside; we can sit on the porch, ride with the windows down in the car; just simple things people enjoy—we will be able to do them again.

There are many jobs for the homeless: keeping the city clean, cutting grass, etc. There are many things people can do. People in charge can form new jobs, or hold town meetings and invite the public. You will be surprised at the knowledge some of the people have if you would give them a chance to speak. They respect you as being a person in charge. It won't make you any less if you listen to the citizens. Most times they give you your job.

TRUST

All of us would like to be able to trust someone. It's hard, but we must learn how to love, respect, and trust. Most people want to do right but sometimes go the way it benefits them most. It seems like it's right to do wrong, so they go for it. We know that wrong in a long period will catch up with us, and it will pay off bad dues. Often people say, "That's true, but do it in the right way." Sometimes people say, "I don't know what I would do if I were in your position"—meaning, they are trying to encourage wrong. Let me encourage you—think for yourself. There are two roads: right and wrong. Be sure the choice you make is yours, and you can live with it in peace.

UNAFRAID—UNAWARE

Most of us are jewels, courageous, respectful, intelligent, lovable, and etc. Everyone is a poet in his or her own way. We think things out in our own way, singing, talking, acting, and just seeing them through. Don't ever wonder how people see you because they take what meets the eye. I'm not saying people are not important, but you are just as important. So, don't be afraid to try some of the things you want. Make sure they are right. We place too much emphasis on what other people think and don't concentrate on ourselves. You may get the opinion of others—but think for yourself. They do not always have the right answer, because they don't know all the facts involved.

Opinion

Everybody has one. Nothing is wrong with sharing. I am very guilty of talking too much, but I talk now because I stayed quiet for about twenty-four years. Maybe I learned to listen by using Plato's school of thought. In a math class in high school, we worked on a project. A group built Plato's school of thought: my brother, S.T., Helen, and classmates. I liked the way those students in Plato's school listened. I think I took that more seriously than the others. I didn't do a lot of work, but I thought about it. I loved being in class with my brother. Not that I was a weak student, I just liked sharing his lesson. My brother Robert use to help me with my lesson. He and S.T. would get my homework when I was a freshman in college. Riding the bus fifty miles a day was too much for me, so I had to go straight to bed so I could make it the next day. One time, I was ill, and Henry was next to me, a handsome, good-looking guy. I talked to him March 15, 1993, on his birthday. He became ill that night. He said, "Mildred, when you know Jesus, you know everything." He was concerned about my health.

My baby brother, Austin, takes care of my car. My big brother, Collins, cooks me fruitcakes at Christmas time. My brother, L.C., lets his wife, Johnnie, fix me good food. I have six sisters. Big sister Beulah has always been supportive to all of us. She was my second-grade teacher. Of course, she was afraid at night that Robert was going to kick her on the ankle for messing with him at school during the day because she was our teacher. Sister, who is called Ms. Mattie, is a famous pie baker. My sister Cora can do anything, just name it. My sister Irene helps us take care of our children and is my assistant pastor at Mt. Evers Cathedral COGIC. She made me look pretty when I was a little girl. My sister Sis (Flora), who lives in California, sent me pretty clothes when I was in high school. I remember a green sweater with a silver chain around the neck. My baby sister, Dean (Ernestine), is like my own child. She was born when my mom was forty-eight years old, so mom was tired and gave her to me. I reared Dean from the time I was ten years old until she was twenty-one years old.

Diamond In The Rough

Our children are just diamonds in the rough waiting to be refined. In this refining, it takes so many things to complete the course. Parents and home are the first factors on the list along with the Christian Arenas, schools, and the community as a whole. Our children have to come so far before they can be responsible for themselves. This is why it takes all of the right things to get them there. Breakfast, lunch, and dinner with the right foods make them strong. Make sure you know your babysitters and visit your children's school because we are shaping the lives of our children. Every phase of this growing-up process is important. Focus on every level of your child's stages of growth. We, as parents, are not perfect, but we can try to be the best we know how.

A diamond in the rough goes through many stages before it is completed. If you notice each stage, you will notice it is the same process children go through. Nothing made is any better than a child. We take plenty of time with material things. Let us do the same with our darling children. You can remake material things, but we can not remake our children. We will suffer a great loss if we turn our backs on them. We are turning our backs on too many things that are important. When we do this, we will be the first to suffer, then others generations after us.

When we think of a diamond in the rough, we know it has to be refined. When that happens, can't we show it off? Just think— a child is more precious than a diamond or gold. When you work with these things, see it as a job. But, when you are working with your children, see it as an act of love.

Failure

We, the society, introduce our children to failures. Children know only what they are exposed or introduced to. We program our children at home, school, etc. It isn't anyone's fault; this is the way it has been. Let them know that people do things differently because there are no two people alike.

I would like to see our school systems non-graded. From Kindergarten to third grade, we should let students learn at their own level without experiencing failure. By this, I mean having goals and objectives that should be met, or levels. Letter grades should also start at the fourth grade. Sometimes I believe this gets in the way of a child's learning. The checklist is a way to take care of grading. This will show whether the child knows or he or she does not. When he or she learns the skills taught, move to another level. A lot of things are not working with us because we don't make them work. Students drop out of school most of the time because they get behind, and there isn't anything in between to get them caught up with the other students. So, they become disgusted and drop out of school. We can stop this if we give children a good foundation in their early years of school. We must understand that children don't do anything at the same time, but that does not say they have a problem. It's true; we group them together and work as closely with them as possible.

When children make slow progress, that does not mean the child has failed. F's, I think, should be done away with. Some teachers use this as a means to an end for them, because the child hasn't understood the subject matter the way they presented it. This could be corrected by letting another teacher take this child. Some teachers go by the book—but there are other methods that can be used that are not written in the manual. This is called common sense. Use some of the everyday experiences in a child's life. A lot of times, we have to be careful about how we phrase a sentence when we speak to a child or anyone. I recall once, I was asked to teach a lesson and leave out all reading. Well, I did just that, and the person became upset. Well, I thought I was doing a good job. The thing I want you to understand is make sure your directions are clear to you before you try to explain them to someone else. Our children are the same way. Let us slow down and make our direction clear so they can understand. Their speed is not important, but it's how well they learn what is being taught.

I am concerned about everybody. Any teacher who gives the whole class F's should stop and consider his or her own ways. That does not mean you are hard; you are just hard for people to understand. If we are going to bridge the gap between home, school, and the community, we are going to have to work together and try to correct our mistakes.

Parents, make sure you visit your child's school to see what you can do to help the teacher with your child, homework, or whatever you need. Teachers, stop getting angry with parents, because they are concerned about their children. Don't take it out on the children just because his or her mom came to school to see how she could help with his or her English lesson or Spanish.

Juvenile Delinquency

Delinquency does occur, but it is hard for me to believe juveniles started the process. We, the parents, are in control first. Too early in the children's lives, we allow them to take control. At first, the children enjoy playing the role of a parent—after a while, all goes downhill for the children and the parents. No one is enjoying anything anymore. Then the parents cry "juvenile delinquency." We, as parents, are the real reasons some of our children become like they are. It is not because we don't know any better. There might be many reasons:

1. Parents don't want to rear children the way you were reared.
2. Other people keep the children for one reason or another.
3. Divided families
4. Grandparents are tired.
5. Schools can't be as responsible for conduct as needed (and children know this).
6. Community and church do not play the role they should.
7. Lack of love
8. Peer pressure

Therefore, our children are not getting the proper guidance from adults that they should. This makes us delinquent instead of the children. Most times, it's hard for a person to find his or her faults. It takes someone else to help you understand where the fault is because all of us need help. Parenting is an important job. When we say it takes the whole world to help our children, we mean that. None of us can be in every place at the same time, but with us united, it will be like the parents are there.

Delinquency gets in the way of our children's learning. I believe that all children can learn. Given the proper environment, guidance, and opportunity, students will exceed our expectations. It is essential that teachers and parents work cooperatively. This would ensure their understanding of student problems and could perhaps curtail them. I truly and strongly believe that the whole is equal to the sum of its parts; therefore, we must work together to develop the whole student. Teachers must be caring and understanding people. My philosophy is, if one thing does not work, try something else and continue until a solution is found. In short, parents must once again assume their respective roles as leaders and role models in the community.

The comprehensive program "Bridging the Gap Between the Home, School, and Community" is a project that I correlated within the Memphis area and throughout the nation. The program has been reviewed by the United States President and the Governor of Tennessee. Goals and objectives of this program continue to be ways to strengthen the relationship between the home, school, and community, as well as parents and teachers.

Community Involvement

Community involvement is a healthy way of life for all of us. Being involved takes away the stressful hours of a person's life. You can find peace any time and place you look for it. When you find yourself feeling sorry for yourself, crying, feeling badly about someone else, saying things that are not pleasing to others, being happy seeing others in trouble, you should get a hold of yourself because stress has set in. So get up and get involved in some kind of activity. If you do not know at first what to do, look around until you find something that makes you happy. There are people waiting for someone to lead them in the right direction.

None of us have all of the answers, but united we can work together and find a solution. Most of the time, it's close by in your church, schools, or somewhere in your community.

It has been a joy for me to write this book. As you read it, if you find things that should be added, feel free to do so. There will be other books after this one. Keep watching out for them. Add this one to your collection and refer to it from time to time.

End